HOW TO WRITE SOCIAL LETTERS

(SPECIAL TECHNIQUES)

HOW TO WRITE SOCIAL LETTERS

(SPECIAL TECHNIQUES)

LILLIAN EICHLER WATSON

INDIANA BOOKS

G-2, 16 Ansari Road, Darya Ganj
New Delhi-110 002

Published by Crest Publishing House
(A Jaico Enterprise)
G-2, 16 Ansari Road,Darya Ganj,
New Delhi - 110 002
sethidel@del6.vsnl.net.in

Exclusively for:
INDIANA
BOOKS

HOW TO WRITE SOCIAL LETTERS

ISBN: 81-242-0097-1

Reprinted: 2005

Printed by:
Gayatri Offset Press
A-66, Sector-2, Noida - 201301

CONTENTS

Chapter I

THE GENERAL RULES OF SOCIAL CORRESPONDENCE

A large part of everyone's correspondence is made up of what might be called the "letters of etiquette." These are the little notes of congratulation and condolence . . . the thank-you's . . . the bread-and-butter letters . . . the invitations and announcements . . . the acceptances and regrets.

It is with these so-called "duty" letters-these many and varied communications of social life-that most people are concerned. For here **correct form** counts more than it does in any other kind of correspondence. Here problems frequently present themselves; it's possible to make glaring errors; and one is likely to be judged more sternly than by ordinary correspondence.

So naturally, it's in writing these "letters of etiquette" that people want most to feel sure of themselves, to know what forms are acceptable according to the best current standards. A friendly letter may be gay and lighthearted as the writer's own personality, as original and different as one pleases. A business letter may be keyed to the special problem at hand. may go so far as to ignore form and precedent entirely to secure the results desired. But a social communication **must he correct.** Whether it's a brief note inviting friends to dinner, or an engraved invitation to an elaborate wedding reception, it must conform to the general rules.

This is simpler than may appear on the surface. Actually, there need never be any problem concerning social correspondence; for the forms are more or less fixed, and are easy to follow. Though these forms may be varied within the limits of good taste, and according to your own particular needs or preferences, it's better to follow them closely than try to be different just for the sake of being different. So confine your originality and unusual ideas to intimate, informal letters to friends. But in social correspondence, be guided by the fixed forms in general use today . . . and by the few simple, basic rules that follow.

ALL SOCIAL CORRESPONDENCE HAS A SPECIFIC PURPOSE

The first thing to bear in mind is that all social communications are for a definite, specific purpose. The important thing is to keep that purpose in mind . . . to let nothing else obtrude ... to convey your message graciously and to the point.

In a friendly letter, of course, you can ramble to your heart's content; the more ground you cover, the more interesting your letter is likely to be! But in a social communication, written for a specific purpose, stay with the subject and don't permit yourself to wander from it.

For example, if it's a letter of thanks, don't write about Aunt Tilly's tulips.

If it's a letter of condolence, don't write even briefly about some unrelated subject.

If it's an invitation, give only the essential facts: the time, the place, the occasion.

Many people make the mistake of combining business and social matters in one letter. That's something you should never do, however much you may be tempted to save time and trouble. **Always keep the specific purpose of the letter in mind, and stay with it.** If you are writing to thank your hostess for a wonderful week end at her country house, don't make that the opportunity to inquire about the Child Aid Society she has organized, to send a check, and to inquire how else you can help. Your note of thanks should be a simple, gracious note of thanks that and nothing more. Your check and your inquiries about the Child Aid Society should be sent as a separate communication.

NEVER INJECT A BUSINESS MATTER INTO A SOCIAL NOTE—LIKE THIS:

Dear Mrs. Compton:

Thanks for a perfect week end! I enjoyed every minute of it.

By the way. I'd like to inquire about the Child Aid Society in which you' are so interested. Can you use any old clothes or toys for the children? I'm enclosing a check for $10.00 to help in the work you are doing.

Again, many thanks for your hospitality!

Sincerely yours,
Martha Winters

ALWAYS SEND TWO SEPARATE COMMUNICATIONS-LIKE THIS:

Dear Mrs. Compton:

I want to thank you for the wonderful week end at Fair Acres. It was just about the most delightful week end I've ever had.

I particularly enjoyed the beach picnic on Saturday I must say you're a **perfect** hostess to have planned so many pleasant things for your guests!

Thanks again for a week end I'll long remember!

Sincerely yours,
Martha Winters

Dear Mrs. Compton:

I'm very much interested in the Child Aid Society you

organized, and would like to know more about it.

Is there any way I can help in the work you are doing? Are you interested in old clothes or toys for the children? I'm sure I can round up a lot of useful things among my friends, if you want them.

In the meantime, I'm enclosing a check for $10.00 my donation to the fund.

Sincerely yours,
Martha Winters

THE DIFFERENCE BETWEEN FORMAL AND INFORMAL CORRESPONDENCE

All social correspondence falls into two general classifications: **formal** and **informal**.

Informal communications are simply handwritten notes, in the **first** person ... like any little note you might write to an acquaintance or friend. They include the many brief notes of congratulation, appreciation, condolence and so forth that we are all called upon to write. They also include notes of invitation, acceptance and regret for simple, informal social affairs like bridge parties, small dinners and luncheons.

A formal invitation implies a large or elaborate social function ... like a church wedding, a ceremonious dinner, an important reception or dance. Formal invitations are usually, but not necessarily, engraved. They are not written in the first person ("I would like you to come to dinner next Wednesday . . .) but in the **third** person ("Mr. and Mrs. Frank B. Hawes cordially invite you to dinner ...). They are not written like ordinary letters, but are arranged in a decorative, irregularly indented form on the page.

EXAMPLE OF INFORMAL SOCIAL NOTE

Dear Mrs. Harris:

Will you come to luncheon on Wednesday, April twenty-seventh at one o'clock? My niece, Doris Fernell, is visiting us, and you have so often mentioned you would like to meet her.

I do hope you will be able to come!

Cordially yours,
Elizabeth K. Benton

EXAMPLE OF FORMAL SOCIAL COMMUNICATION

Dr. and Mrs. Thomas Matthew Benton
request the pleasure of your company
at a dinner dance for their niece
Miss Doris Female
Wednesday, the fourth of May
at eight o'clock
Hotel Pierre

Naturally the type of invitation you send out depends entirely on the type of affair. You wouldn't send formal engraved invitations for a simple little dinner party attended by just a few friends. Nor would you send informal handwritten notes to a long list of people invited to an elaborate church or hotel wedding. Good taste requires that the invitation **suit the occasion**.

In the past it was permissible to use visiting cards for invitations, when one didn't wish to be formal or informal but somewhere midway between the two. The procedure was to write the occasion and the date in the lower left corner of the card, as follows:

Dinner at eight
May the fifth

The card was then slipped into an envelope and mailed,

without further comment. Though one still occasionally sees this type of invitation, it is no longer generally used; and is, in fact, poor taste and should be avoided.

WHAT YOU SHOULD KNOW ABOUT INFORMAL CORRESPONDENCE

1. Don't be fooled by the word "informal." The stationery you used for your notes of invitation, acceptance, regret-for your messages of condolence or congratulation—should be **important-looking**. Don't use tinted or decorated note paper; that's for your intimate, personal correspondence only. Don't use business or club stationery; that's definitely bad taste. Use only good quality plain white note paper of standard size. Double sheets are more impressive than single sheets for social use; and it's considered better form to get all the message on one page than to carry it over.
2. Informal social notes are usually brief, and should be handwritten. Some people prefer to type all their correspondence, including social notes; and although it's not actually incorrect to do so, it's more **gracious** to write a note of sympathy or thanks by hand. Invitations, of course, should not be typed; a handwritten invitation is much more personal and friendly.
3. Make it a point never to put off writing your necessary social correspondence. A message of sympathy or appreciation, long delayed, loses much of its effectiveness. So attend to your little "duty" notes promptly! **Don't put off till tomorrow what you can write today.**
4. Be sure that any note of invitation you send out is explicit and **complete.** Don't leave anything to the imagination. Give the occasion, the place, the date. the time. For example don't say "I'd like you and Tom to come to dinner next Wednesday." Say. "I'd like you and Tom to come to dinner on Wednesday. June tenth."

5. Evening invitations, whether formal or informal, must include both husband and wife—unless, of course, it's a "stag." An informal invitation is addressed to the wife alone, for herself and her husband. The envelope is addressed to "Mrs. Thomas M. Benton"but the invitation makes specific mention of the husband. For example:

   Dear Betty:

   We are planning a little dinner to celebrate our tenth anniversary, and of course we want you and Tom to come. It's next Friday, June eighth, at seven o'clock.

   I do hope you can make it, as Jim and I are looking forward with great pleasure to seeing you both.

   Affectionately yours,
   Rosalind

6. An informal note of invitation like the one above is answered the same way—by means of a brief, handwritten note. It's written by the wife, for her husband and herself; and though the envelope is addressed to the hostess alone, the names of **both** host and hostess should be mentioned in the acknowledgment. For example:

   Dear Rosalind:

   Tom and I are delighted to accept your invitation to dinner on Friday, June eighth, at seven o'clock. Thanks for asking us.

   We are greatly. complimented that you and Jim should have asked us to share in such a very **special** celebration as your tenth anniversary!

   Cordially yours,
   Betty,

7. Bear in mind that an invitation is a compliment and deserves a prompt and gracious reply. Always try to answer an informal note of invitation within twentyfour hours if you can—but certainly within three days at the most. Your hostess may want to make other

arrangements if you can not accept. Always answer by note if you are invited by note. There are times, of course, when it may be necessary to telephone your acceptance or regret. But a note in your own handwriting is more courteous . . . and therefore more desirable.

8. Your response to an invitation should be a **definite** acceptance or regret. Don't keep your hostess in doubt with such vague comments as:

   "I hope I can come."
   "I'll try my best to come."
   "I'll come if I'm in town."
   "I'll come if the baby is well."

   State definitely that you are coming or that you are **not** coming, so your hostess can make her plans accordingly. She may want to invite someone else if you can't come.

9. When you write a note accepting an invitation, be sure to express pleasure at having been invited. It's the gracious thing to do. If you cannot accept the invitation, express your disappointment and regret ... and give the reason for not accepting. Don't just say, "I'm sorry I can't come to your luncheon next Tuesday" . . . but "I'm sorry I can't come to your luncheon next Tuesday because that's the day Bob gets home from school." Make your note cordial and appreciative, but **stay with the subject:** discuss the matter of the luncheon invitation only. Don't be tempted to write about the fine marks your son got at school, or the way you had his room redecorated as a surprise.

10. In accepting an invitation, always repeat essential data such as the day of the week, the date, the hour and so forth. For example, don't just write "I'll be delighted to attend your luncheon . . ." but "I'll be delighted to attend your luncheon on Thursday. May tenth, at one o'clock." This enables the hostess to correct any mistake in date or time that either you or she may have made.

WHAT YOU SHOULD KNOW ABOUT FORMAL CORRESPONDENCE

1. Formal correspondence may seem difficult and forbidding to the uninitiated; but actually it should present no real problems. For its very phraseology is standard and fixed, and entails less composition than the simplest little informal note. As a rule, formal invitations and announcements—issued only for elaborate and important affairs—are **engraved** on double sheets of fine quality white paper, in keeping with the dignity of the occasion. They may also be, **handwritten** in which case the wording, spacing and arrangement should follow, the engraved forms exactly. Formal communications should **not** be printed; they should either be engraved in the traditional way, or written carefully by hand.
2. The style of lettering used in an engraved invitation is entirely a matter of personal choice. Script, gothic and shaded roman are the most popular choices; but this and other details of engraved forms are best decided in conjunction with your stationer or engraver. Either **plain** or **paneled** double sheets may be used; and though a family crest or coat of arms may be embossed without color at the top of the sheet, remember that here—as in **all** correspondence—simplicity is the keynote of good taste. lie engraved form is decorative enough in itself without the use of monograms or other personal devices.
3. There are two distinct types of formal invitation. Both are correct, and either may be used . . . depending upon your own personal preference. The first is engraved **in full**, with the generalised phrase "request the pleasure of your company" instead of the specific name of the guest. Here is a typical example of such an invitation:

Dr. and Mrs. Thomas Matthew Benton
request the pleasure of your company
on the Twenty-fifth Anniversary of their marriage
on Thursday, the tenth of June
from four until seven o'clock
The Park Lane
New York

The second has a **blank space** in which the name of the individual guest is written by hand. This fill-in type of invitation is somewhat more personal, and therefore many people prefer it:

Dr. and Mrs. Thomas Matthew Benton
request the pleasure of
Mr. and Mrs. Frank North's
company at a dance
on Friday, the twelfth of October
at ten o'clock
The Sherry-Netherland

4. No abbreviations, no nicknames, no informal phraseology of any kind are used in an engraved communication. Names should be spelled out in full, without the use of initials. The date, the time, even the year when it is given, are all spelled out instead of being written numerically. House numbers should be spelled out when short, but may be written numerically when long. Thus you would use "Ten Park Avenue" but "428 Ocean Drive." Telephone numbers are never used on engraved invitations.
5. The phrase "request the **honor of your presence"** is used for wedding invitations, and especially church wedding. "Request the **pleasure of your company**" is used for dinners, dances and similar functions. "Honour" and "favour" are British forms of spelling to which many still cling; but we prefer the American style of spelling, without the **u,** and recommend its use.

6. Formal invitations to dinners, dances, luncheons should be sent out three weeks in advance. This gives the hostess time to fill in, in case of regrets. Wedding, invitations are generally mailed a month in advance. **Announcements** are sent out the day of the event or after it, not before.
7. A formal invitation should always include husband and wife; neither should be invited without the other unless it's a stag, or an afternoon function for ladies only (such as a luncheon or tea). If a daughter is included in the invitation, her name is written on the envelope below that of her parents. If two or more daughters are included, their names may either appear on the envelope below their parents' names; or they may be addressed separately—with individual invitations to each, or one invitation addressed jointly to "The Misses Howell" or "Misses Mary and Joan Howell." A young son may be included by adding his name to the envelope; but an adult male member of a family is invited by separate invitation. Brothers may be invited as "Messrs. John and Stephen Howell."
8. Surely it should not be necessary to have to ask for a reply to an invitation! But in these hurried and careless times, it is often advisable to do so. If a reply is requested, one of the following forms should be used. Its proper position is in the lower left corner of the invitation, engraved in a somewhat smaller-size lettering than the rest of the message written in by hand if it is a handwritten communication :

   Please reply
   An answer is requested
   The favor of a reply is requested
   Please address reply to (address)
   Please send response to (address)
   Kindly reply to (address)

One of the most commonly used forms is "R.s.v.p." This is the abbreviation for **"Respondez s'il vous plait"** which is French for "Reply if you please." The abbreviation frequently appears in capitals (R.S.V.P.), but to he strictly correct only the first letter should be a capital and the other letters should be small (R.s.v.p.). While this form of request for a reply is very popular and widely used, our own preference is for a simple English phrase like "Please reply."

9. The acceptance or regret of a formal invitation should be in **your own handwriting**. Don't use a printed form, to be filled in as the occasion requires. Such ready-made response to an invitation is in poor taste. Nor do we recommend the practice of sending a visiting card with "Accepts" or "Regrets" written in the corner—once good form, but now looked upon as a rudeness. Your reply should be written out carefully, in exactly the same phraseology as the invitation. . . . and in the same irregularly indented form. It should be written on the first page of a double sheet of good quality plain white note paper, approximating as closely as possible the appearance of the invitation. Here, for example, is how the invitation of Dr. and Mrs. Benton on page 10 should be acknowledged.

Mr. and Mrs. Frank North

accept with pleasure

Dr. and Mrs. Thomas M. Benton's

invitation to a dance

on Friday, the twelfth of October

at ten o'clock

The Sherry-Netherland

This would be in your own handwriting, of course— but placed and arranged as above, following the form of the engraved invitation. And no matter how well you know your hostess, or how eagerly you would Profor writing a cordial, friendly little note in reply ... resist the temptation! For good social usage requires that a formal communication always be answered **in kind.**

10. Notice that the acknowledgment above is from both Mr. and Mrs. North-not-Mrs. North alone. And notice also that the acknowledgment, is made to **both** Dr. and Mrs. Benton. However, the envelope in which the acknowledgment is mailed should be addressed to Mrs. Benton only. When an invitation includes another member of the family, the acknowledgment should also include that person's name. For example, if the Norths' daughter, Sandra, was also invited to the Bentons' dance, the acknowledgment would read:

Mr. and Mrs. Frank North
Miss Sandra North
accept with pleasure
and so forth

11. If a husband and wife are invited to a formal dinner or reception, and the husband is unable to attend, the wife should send regrets for both. The reason for the regret is not always given in a formal acknowledgment; but it is more courteous to do so. For example, if Mr. North is out of town Mrs. North might write as follows to Mrs. Benton. who could then invite her alone. or not. as she sees fit:

Owing to Mr. North's
absence from town on business
Mrs. Frank North
regrets she is unable to accept
Dr. and Mrs. Thomas M. Benton's
kind invitation
for Friday, the twelfth of October

12. Occasionally an invitation must be recalled due to illness a death in the family, or perhaps a broken engagement. Such recalls must go out as quickly as possible; and as there is no time to have them engraved, they should be carefully handwritten in formal phraseology—but in this case, not necessarily formal spacing. The reason for the recall of the invitation may or may not be given, at the discretion of the persons most involved; but of course it's always more courteous to make an explanation. For example:

Dr. and Mrs. Thomas Matthew
Benton regret that, owing to the
sudden illness of their son, they
are obliged to recall their
invitations for Friday. the twelfth
of October.

❑ ❑ ❑ ❑ ❑

Chapter II

DINNER INVITATIONS AND ACKNOWLEDGMENTS

Engraved third-person invitations are a last lingering reminder of the extreme formality that once existed in social life. Comparatively few of us have occasion to issue such invitations today. except for certain special functions like weddings. In fact, there is considerably less formality in social life today than ever before in the past. Invitations are now frequently made by telephone, and even more casually when friends chance to meet. But as long as there are still occasions that call for formal announcements or invitations—and still the need to reply to such communications properly—you should be familiar with the forms that good usage has established and tradition preserved.

One occasion that still calls for a strictly formal invitation is the elaborate, ceremonious dinner. This may be a dinner to honor a famous or special guest, to introduce a debutante daughter to society, or perhaps to celebrate a wedding anniversary. If the dinner is given at a club or hotel, the invitations are usually engraved. If given at home, the invitations may still be engraved; but frequently they are written by hand, especially when the dinner is a small one. But bear in mind that when formal invitations are written by hand, they do not deviate from the traditional form: they follow the wording and spacing of the engraved form exactly.

Now obviously, the type of invitation you send out does not determine the kind of dinner party you give. It's the other way around: the **type of dinner** determines the invitation. If you are planning a simple little dinner for a few friends—and you habitually call those friends on the telephone and say, "How about coming for dinner next Thursday"—that's the way to keep on doing it! But if you are planning a formal dinner, you must plan on formal invitations as well. Such invitations must be mailed two or three weeks in advance; and if you have them engraved, that takes another week or two—so you can see you need to make your and well ahead of time. And be very sure you give the correct information to the engraver, for mistakes in spelling, in date, place, hour, etc. cannot be corrected once the form is run off.

ENGRAVED INVITATION TO A FORMAL DINNER

Dr. and Mrs. Thomas Matthew Benton
request the pleasure of your company
at dinner
on Thursday, September the twentieth
at eight o'clock
250 Park Avenue

ENGRAVED FILL-IN-TYPE OF DINNER INVITATION

Dr. and Mrs. Thomas Matthew Benton
request the pleasure of
Mr. and Mrs. Robert B. Clark's
company at dinner
on Thursday, September the twentieth
at eight o'clock
250 Park Avenue

HANDWRITTEN INVITATION TO A FORMAL DINNER

Dr. and Mrs. Thomas Matthew Benton
request the pleasure of
Mr. and Mrs. Robert B. Clark's
company at dinner
on Thursday, September the twentieth
at eight o'clock.

Handwritten invitations, as a rule, do not include the address...as most note paper used for social correspondence already has the address at the top. But cards or note paper to be engraved do **not** have the address at the top, and it must therefore be included in the body Of the invitation.

Don't use "Mr. & Mrs." in social correspondence. Make it a point to spell out the word "and" between "Mr. and Mrs." in- all social correspondence. The symbol & is for business correspondence only.

ALWAYS RESPOND PROMPTLY TO A DINNER INVITATION

A dinner invitation is one of the highest forms of social courtesy. It's a compliment to you and should be treated as such, being acknowledged promptly and with a definite acceptance or regret.

A formal invitation should be acknowledged within twenty-four hours, if possible. That gives the hostess time to make other arrangements if you send regrets. Don't reply with an informal note. as that suggests you are unfamiliar with good social usage. Follow the exact wording of the invitation, writing on the first page of your note paper only, and centering the message attractively so that it not only **reads** but **looks** formal. Here, for example, is the way an acceptance of the invitation above should look:

30 Sutton Place
Mr. and Mrs. Roger B. Clark
accept with pleasure
Dr. and Mrs. Thomas M. Benton's
kind invitation for dinner
on Thursday, September twentieth
at eight o'clock

There is a growing tendency nowadays to write formal acknowledgments without indented margins, following only the wording and not the arrangement of the invitation. There's no real objection to writing your acknowledgment this way, if you find the style more to your taste and liking. But the very best social usage still calls for decorative spacing; and though the following **may** be used. the form shown above is still preferred:

> Mr. and Mrs. Roger B. Clark accept
> with pleasure Dr. and Mrs. Thomas
> M. Benton's kind invitation for
> dinner on Thursday. September the
> twentieth, at eight o'clock

If you cannot accept a dinner invitation, it's always courteous to give the reason why in your response. Formerly an acknowledgment was all that was required—no explanation. But that is now looked upon as rude and ungracious according to today's standards. The following are typical "regrets" to a formal dinner invitation written by hand, of course, on your best white note paper:

Mr. and Mrs. Robert B. Clark
regret that a previous engagement
prevents their accepting
Dr. and Mrs. Thomas M. Benton's
kind invitation for dinner
on Thursday, September the twentieth

Mr. and Mrs. Robert B. Clark
regret exceedingly that they
are unable to accept
Dr. and Mrs. Thomas M. Benton's
kind invitation for dinner
on Thursday, September the twentieth
owing to illness in the family

An acceptance always requires the repetition of both the date and the hour to prevent the possibility of a misunderstanding. But a regret requires the repetition of the date only.

DINNER IN HONOR OF A SPECIAL GUEST OR GUESTS

Invitation

Dr. and Mrs. Thomas Matthew Benton
request the pleasure of
Mr. and Mrs. Roger B. Clark's
company at dinner
on Thursday, September the twentieth
at eight o'clock
to meet Mr. John T. Alden
250 Park Avenue

Acceptance

Mr. and Mrs. Roger B. Clark
accept with pleasure
Dr. and Mrs. Thomas M. Benton's
kind invitation for dinner
on Thursday, September the twentieth
at eight o'clock
to meet Mr. John T. Alden

Regret

Mr. and Mrs. Roger B. Clark
regret that a previous engagement
prevents their accepting
Dr. and Mrs. Thomas M. Benton's
kind invitation for dinner
on Thursday, September the twentieth
to meet Mr. John T. Alden

Frequently, when the guests of honor are persons of particular importance or prominence, their names are placed at the top of the invitation. The words **"To Meet"** may be used as shown; or the entire phrase, **"To meet**

General; and Mrs. Wayne R. Pratt" may be used as the first line.

Invitation

To meet
General and Mrs. Wayne R. Pratt
Dr. and Mrs. Thomas Matthew Benton
request the pleasure of your company
at dinner
at the Ritz-Carlton
on Thursday, September the twentieth
at half past seven o'clock

Acceptance

To meet
General and Mrs. Wayne R. Pratt
Mr. and Mrs. Roger B. Clark
accept with pleasure
Dr. and Mrs. Thomas M. Benton's
kind invitation for dinner
at the Ritz-Carlton
on Thursday, September the twentieth
at half past seven o'clock

Regret

Mr. and Mrs. Roger B. Clark
regret that owing to illness
they are unable to accept
Dr. and Mrs. Thomas M. Benton's
kind invitation for dinner
on Thursday, September the twentieth
to meet General and Mrs. Wayne R. Pratt

DINNER TO CELEBRATE A SPECIAL OCCASION

When a dinner is given to celebrate some special occasion—like a wedding anniversary or a daughter's debut—that purpose is usually stated in the invitation.

Invitation

Mr. and Mrs. Paul Preston
request the pleasure of your company
at dinner on the
Twenty-fifth Anniversary of their marriage
Wednesday, the fifth of June
at seven o'clock
20 Lake Drive

Acceptance

Mr. and Mrs. Robert G. Scully
accept with pleasure
Mr. and Mrs. Paul Preston's
invitation for dinner
on the Twenty-fifth Anniversary of their marriage
Wednesday, the fifth of June
at seven o'clock

Regret

Mr. and Mrs. Robert G. Scully
regret exceedingly that they
are unable to accept
Mr. and Mrs. Paul Preston's
invitation for dinner on the
Twenty-fifth Anniversary of their marriage
Wednesday, the fifth of June
owing to serious illness in the family

DINNER FOR A DEBUTANTE DAUGHTER

Invitation

Dr. and Mrs. Thomas Matthew Benton
request the pleasure of your company
at dinner
in honor of their daughter
Miss Anita Benton
on Saturday, the fifteenth of November
at eight o'clock
The Waldorf-Astoria

Please send reply to
250 Park Avenue

Acceptance

Mr. and Mrs. Carl Whitney
accept with pleasure
Dr. and Mrs. Thomas M. Benton's
invitation for dinner
in honor of their daughter
Miss Anita Benton
on Saturday, the fifteenth of November
at eight o'clock
The Waldorf-Astoria

Regret

Mr. and Mrs. Carl Whitney
regret that they are unable to accept
Dr. and Mrs. Thomas M. Benton's
invitation for dinner
in honor of their daughter
Miss Anita Benton
on Saturday, the fifteenth of November
as they will be abroad at that time

DINNER FOLLOWED BY CONCERT OR OPERA

Formal dinner invitations sometimes include an invitation

to a play, opera, concert or lecture later on in the evening. As only a comparatively few guests can be invited to share such an evening, the invitations are almost always written by hand. Nowadays, of course, the trend is toward much simpler and less pretentious entertaining of small groups than this. Most of us would be more inclined to have an informal little dinner, either at home or at a restaurant or hotel, before going on to the theater or opera; and we would write simple, little notes to our guests, or even invite them by telephone. But for those who still cling to the old social traditions. and who like to entertain even small groups of friends occasionally with old-fashioned formality, we include these examples of correct invitations for "dinner and afterward."

Invitation

Dr. and Mrs. Thomas Matthew Benton
request the pleasure of
Mr. and Mrs. Peter Kenway's
company at dinner
on Wednesday, April the eighteenth
at seven o'clock
and at the Leonard Berstein recital afterward

or

Dr. and Mrs. Thomas Matthew Benton
request the pleasure of
Mr. and Mrs. Peter Kenwa 's
company for dinner and the opera
on Wednesday, April the eighteenth
at seven o'clock

Please reply to
250 Park Avenue

Acceptance

Mr. and Mrs. Peter Kenway
accept with pleasure
Dr. and Mrs. Thomas M. Benton's
kind, invitation for dinner
on Wednesday, April the eighteenth
at seven o'clock
and for-the Leonard Bernstein recital afterward

Mr. and Mrs. Peter Kenway
accept with pleasure
Dr. and Mrs. Thomas M. Benton's
invitation for dinner and the opera
on Wednesday, April the eighteenth
at seven o'clock

Regret

Mr. and Mrs. Peter Kenway
regret exceedingly that a previous engagement
prevents their accepting
Dr. and Mrs. Thomas M. Benton's
kind invitation for dinner
on Wednesday, April the eighteenth
and for the Leonard Bernstein recital afterward

Mr. and Mrs. Peter Kenway
regret that they are
unable to accept
Dr. and Mrs. Thomas M. Benton's
invitation for dinner and the opera
on Wednesday, April the eighteenth
owing to a previous engagement

DINNER BY SONS AND DAUGHTERS IN HONOR OF PARENTS

When a group of children, married and unmarried, give a formal dinner in honour of their parents' silver or golden wedding anniversary, an invitation like the following is the most practical. It is issued in the names of all the sons and daughters, with a reply requested in the name of one person in the group selected to handle this part of the arrangements

In honor of the
Fiftieth Wedding Anniversary of
Mr. and Mrs. James Gray
their sons and daughters
request the pleasure of
Mr. and Mrs. Thomas M. Benton's
company at dinner
on Friday, the sixth of June
at eight o'clock
The Hampshire House

Kindly send reply to
Miss Joyce Gray
Tuxedo Park, New York

A person receiving the invitation above is required to make formal acknowledgment to all the sons and daughters; but the envelope is addressed only to "Miss Joyce Gray." as requested. The acceptance or regret should be carefully written by hand, on good quality white note paper, and mailed within twenty-four hours after receipt of the invitation:

Acceptance

Mr. and Mrs. Thomas M. Benton
accept with great pleasure
the invitation of
the sons and daughters
of Mr. and Mrs. James Gray
for dinner
in honor of their parents'
Fiftieth Wedding Anniversary
on Friday, the sixth of June
at eight o'clock
at the Hampshire House

If you prefer to write your acknowledgment without the indented margins, you may do so—as previously mentioned. But remember that to be socially correct, **the wording must follow the wording of the invitation.**

Regret

Mr. and Mrs. Thomas M. Benton
regret extremely that
they are unable to accept
the invitation of
the sons and daughters of
Mr. and Mrs. James Gray
for dinner
in honour of their parents'
Fiftieth Wedding Anniversary
on Friday, the sixth of June
owing to a previous engagement

These who are especially courteous, and social-minded send congratulations on the day of the dinner; and later write a note to the guests of honor (in this case, the parents) — explaining why they were unable to be present and how sorry they were to have missed it.

HOW TO POSTPONE OR CANCEL FORMAL DINNER INVITATIONS

It frequently happens that a dinner party must be canceled or postponed, sometimes almost at the, very last minute, due to illness or other circumstances. If there is time, the hostess writes a formal note . . . assuming, of course, that this was to have been a formal dinner and engraved invitations were sent out. If there isn't time for a note, the hostess (or someone representing her) should telephone or telegraph all guests at once.

The following examples show how formal dinner invitations are usually recalled or postponed. Because of the nature of the communication, these notes—though in the third person—are not, as a rule, written with indented spacing. It is considered somewhat better taste, in this particular instance, to eliminate the decorative arrangement—and write the notes as follows:

> Dr. and Mrs. Thomas Matthew Benton regret that, owing to the severe illness of their son, the dinner arranged for next Friday must be postponed.

> Mr. and Mrs. Frank B. Hawes wish to announce that the dinner planned for next Tuesday, in honor of their niece, is temporarily postponed due to illness in the family.

> Mr. and Mrs. Paul Preston regret that damages done to their house by a recent fire make it necessary to postpone the dinner arranged for April third until May fifth at the same time.

> Mr. and Mrs. Carl Whitney wish to announce that the dinner planned for next Saturday has been postponed until the following Saturday, October the tenth, owing to the fact that Mr. Whitney has been unexpectedly called out of town.

> Mr. and Mrs. James Carter, Jr. regret that they are obliged to recall their invitations for Thursday, the second of November, because of the death of their nephew, Mr. Henry Pierce Lowe.

> Owing to injuries sustained in a recent automobile accident, Mr. and Mrs. Curtis Henning regret that they must cancel their dinner planned for Wednesday, October the eighth.

Mr. and Mrs. Peter Kenway regret that they are obliged to recall their invitations for next Thursday, due to unavoidable circumstances.

The last of the above is the least courteous, for it offers no explanation. Bear in mind that these are **formal** notes, correct only when engraved invitations have been sent. For canceling or postponing a simple, informal dinner, you would write a personal note of explanation, or you would telephone.

HOW TO BREAK A FORMAL DINNER ENGAGEMENT

Sometimes it's the **guest** and not the hostess who is obliged to make a last-minute change of plans due to illness or other, circumstances. It goes without saying, of course, that a dinner engagement should never be broken unless there is a very good reason for it. And if there is such a reason, it calls for **prompt action**— either by letter or telephone. The hostess must be informed fully and at once of the circumstances which present the guest from being present as planned.

Dear Mrs. Benton:

Mr. Carter has been called to Philadelphia on account of the sudden illness of his sister. We are very anxious about her, and I am, sure you will understand why it is impossible for either of us to attend your dinner party next Tuesday.

We are both extremely sorry to break our engagement at this late date; and hope you and Dr. Benton will forgive us.

Sincerely yours.
Florence Carter

Dear Mrs. Whitney:

I have just learned that my, sister, who lives in

Rochester, has been seriously injured in an automobile accident. Mr. Hunt and I are leaving at once to be with her.

I'm sure we cannot be back in time for your dinner on Thursday, and hope you will understand and forgive us under the circumstances.

With many regrets.

Sincerely yours.
Alice T. Hunt

INVITING A FRIEND TO FILL AN EMPTY PLACE AT DINNER

When a hostess finds herself short one dinner guest, due to the fact that someone was unable to come at the last minute, the usual thing is to call on a friend to fill in the gap. If time is short, she telephones; otherwise she writes a note frankly explaining the situation and askings the friend to fill in as a special favor. It's not an easy letter to write. No one likes to play "second fiddle"—to be invited only because someone else was unable to come. But it's much better to put it on this frank basis than to invite someone only a day or two ahead of time **without** an explanation. That sort of last-minute invitation fools no one, and is much more likely to injure sensitive feelings than a straightforward note like the following:

Dear Frank:

If you have no other plans for this Thursday night, the twelfth. will you join my dinner party? One of my guests has just telephoned that he can't come because of illness.

So you see, Frank, I'm putting it to you very honestly! I need another guest—and Jim and I can think of no one we'd rather have than you. Will you overlook the informality of this rather flurried invitation and make us both very happy by accepting?

Sincerely yours,
Laura Winston

There is usually no time to respond by letter to such an invitation. It's more likely to be acknowledged by telephone. But if there **is** time to write, the letter should be especially friendly and cordial. The invitation should either be accepted graciously . . . or a very good reason for not accepting it should be given.

Dear Laura:

I guess I should be sorry for that chap who is ill ... but I'm not at all! I'm very glad of the opportunity to enjoy another of your delightful dinners.

So you and Jim can count me in, and thanks for asking me!

Yours sincerely,
Frank Lennon

Dear Laura:

I wish I could accept your invitation for Thursday night! I know I'd Enjoy it as I have always enjoyed your charming dinner parties. But unfortunately I am leaving on a business trip tomorrow, and will be far from New York by Thursday.

My very best to you and Jim, and thanks for thinking of me!

Sincerely yours,
Frank Lennon

INFORMAL DINNER INVITATIONS AND HOW TO ANSWER THEM

The invitations and acknowledgments we have been discussing up to this point are for elaborately formal and "special occasion" dinners only. But the average person today entertains **informal**, and has far more occasion to write simple little notes of invitation than to send out engraved social forms.

However, though informal notes provide much greater

latitude than formal third-person invitations ... they, too, follow a fairly fixed pattern. They are usually written in two brief paragraphs; and however the words may vary, the message always remains essentially this: "Will you come to dinner on a certain date, at a certain time?

A note inviting people to dinner is always written by the hostess for her husband and herself. It is addressed to "Mrs." only, not to "Mr. and Mrs.'—but the note should include-mention of the husband, otherwise it is a discourtesy to him. For example:

Dear Mrs. Jennings:

Will you and Mr. Jennings have dinner with us on Tuesday, the fifth of May, at seven o'clock?

It's a long time since we have had the pleasure of seeing you, and we do hope you can come.

Sincerely yours,
Elizabeth K. Benton

The person who removed such a note should answer it promptly, and with a **definite** acceptance or regret. It should not be a vague or conditional response, such as:

"I'd like to come if I can; it depends on whether or not Paul gets back from Baltimore in time." That leaves the hostess "up a tree," so to speak. The answer should be a specific, "Yes, we'll be delighted to come! "—or "So sorry! We can't come because . . ."

The acceptance of any invitation, of course, should be an implied "Thank you"—graciously and unmistakably expressed. The words may say it any way you like; but the tone or spirit of your note must clearly convey the impression that you are pleased to have been invited that you are glad to accept . . . and that you are looking forward to the occasion with eagerness.

Dear Mrs. Benton:

Mr. Jennings and I will be delighted to dine with you on

Tuesday, the fifth of May, at seven o'clock. How very nice of you to ask us!

We are both looking forward with great pleasure to seeing you and Dr. Benton again.

Very sincerely yours,
Susan Jennings

If it's necessary to decline a dinner invitation, the note should be very carefully written to avoid giving offense. The reason for not being able to accept should be given; and it's always courteous to say how sorry you are, and to suggest how very hard you tried to overcome the obstacle that stood in the way. The tone of the letter should be one of sincere regret:

Dear Mrs. Benton:

I've been putting off this note until the last possible moment, hoping and hoping Mr. Jennings would get back from Baltimore in time for your dinner party. But now I must regretfully write that he'll still be out of town on Tuesday, the fifth, and we therefore cannot accept your kind invitation for dinner on that day.

It was sweet of you to ask us; and I know Mr. Jennings will be as sorry as I am to miss an evening with you and Dr. Benton. We know how delightful such evenings at your house usually are!

Sincerely yours,
Susan Jennings

The easiest way out of an invitation you do not care to accept is to plead a previous engagement. That is always an acceptable excuse. But be sure your note. however brief, sounds as though you are really sorry:

Dear Mrs. Benton:

I just can't tell you how sorry Mr. Jennings and I are that we cannot dine with you on Tuesday, the fifth of May.

Unfortunately we already have an engagement for that evening.

Thank you for asking us, and we hope you will give us the opportunity to say "yes" some other time.

Sincerely yours,
Susan Jennings

Obviously the above invitations and acknowledgments are not intended for -intimate friends. They are the kind of notes you would write to people you know **casually**, not closely . . . people you invite **occasionally**, for purely social reasons, not **frequently** because you love them and enjoy being with them.

But bear in mind that even to an intimate friend, an invitation should be an **invitation**—not a minor detail lost in a long account of local news, family gossip and other idle writing! An invitation seems much more important to the person who receives it when it's sent as a special and separate communication instead of just part of a chatty letter.

Here, for example, is how you might invite a close friend to dinner **correctly,** yet **cordially:**

Dear Ruth:

Tom and I are having some very special friends here for dinner on Thursday, October second. Naturally the party wouldn't be complete without you and Bill!

We hope you can come, as we are planning to show the movies we made in Nassau, and we know you and Bill are thinking of going there this winter.

Dinner is at seven, as usual. We'll be looking for you two charming people at that time, so don't disappoint us!

Affectionately yours,
Betty

Not even close friendship permits of laxity in the matter

of response to a dinner invitation. A note like the above should be acknowledged promptly, and in kind. Although many people now prefer the convenience of telephoning a response, it's always better form to **answer by note when invited by note.** This applies to invitations from personal friends as well as those you know less intimately.

Dear Betty:

How could we even **think** of turning down the prospect of another delightful evening with you and Tom? Of course we'll be there on Thursday, October second —promptly at seven!

Bill and I are both excited about seeing those Nassau pictures. We think that's where we're going for our vacation this winter., so it will be wonderful seeing your pictures and getting a "preview" of the island.

Thanks for asking us, Betty. We're certainly looking, forward to next Tuesday!

Affectionately yours,
Ruth

There's an old familiar saying: "You never need to explain to a friend." But that doesn't apply to dinner invitations! If you refuse an invitation, You must explain why—even to a friend. Especially to a friend!

Dear Betty:

What a shame! We won't be able to come to your dinner party on Thursday because that's the day We're having the Gilmores **here** for dinner.

You remember I told you about Mr. Gilmore last week. He's one of Bill's most important clients. If it were anyone else, I'd alter my plans—even at the very last moment—rather than miss an evening with you and Tom! But I just can't do that with the Gilmores, Betty, I'm sure you understand.

Bill and I would certainly like to see those Nassau

pictures, as we think that's where we're going this winter. Will you give us a private showing some time? Just say when and will be there!

Have a good time on Tuesday. I certainly wish we could be with you!

Affectionately,
Ruth

INVITING FRIENDS TO DINNER AND THE THEATER

Notes of invitation are often quite brief, these busy days. and no one thinks anything of it. An invitation for dinner and the theater is frequently just a hurried line or two from one friend to another. But that doesn't necessarily mean the note is curt or abrupt. It's just written fast, as so many things must be now.

Dear Ann:

We have four seats for the opening of the O'Neill play this Friday, the tenth. Will you and John join us here for dinner at seven sharp; and then go on with us later to the play? We'll be looking for you Friday night, so don't disappoint us!

Fondly,
Doris

Acceptance

Dear Doris:

Delighted! We'll be there Friday at seven, and go with you afterward to the theater. How wonderful of you and Frank to ask us!

With affection,
Ann

Regret

Dear Doris:

I think you'd better ask some other couple for Friday. John's in Washington and won't be back for another week. Wait till he hears what a wonderful evening he missed with you and Frank! Thanks for asking us. Doris. I'm certainly sorry we can't say "yes"!

Affectionately yours
Ann

WHEN A DAUGHTER ACTS AS HOSTESS

In a motherless home, a young daughter is often required to act as hostess for her father. She does not send out dinner invitations in her own name, but always includes mention of her father and makes it clear that she is acting for him, at his request.

Dear Mrs. Everett:

Father wishes me to ask if you and Mr. Everett can dine with us on Monday, March the fifth, at seven o'clock.

We hope you can come, and look forward to seeing you.

Sincerely yours,
Marcia Curtis

The acknowledgment must go to the **daughter**, not the father. The response to any invitation must go to the person who writes it.

Acceptance

Dear Miss Curtis:

Mr. Everett and I are delighted to accept your father's invitation for dinner on Monday, March the fifth, at seven o'clock.

We send our affectionate greetings to both of you.

Sincerely yours,
Janet P. Everett

Regret

Dear Miss Curtis:

I regret that a previous engagement prevents us from accepting your father's kind invitation for dinner on, Monday, March the fifth.

Please tell him that Mr. Everett and I thank him for asking us, and we are very sorry indeed that we cannot come.

Sincerely yours,
Janet P. Everett

NOTE TO RECALL AN INFORMAL DINNER INVITATION

Dear Mrs. Jennings:

I have just learned that my son, who is at school in Massachusetts, was injured in a basketball game. Although the injury is not serious, Dr. Benton and I feel we must go to him at once; and we are leaving tomorrow morning.

Under the circumstances, we must recall our dinner invitations for Tuesday, the fifth of May ... and plan on a later date for our party.

I'm sure that you and Mr. Jennings will understand our anxiety, and will forgive this last-minute change in plans.

Sincerely yours,
Elizabeth K. Benton

NOTE TO BREAK AN INFORMAL DINNER ENGAGEMENT

Dear Mrs. Benton:

I'm so very sorry to have to write you this letter! After accepting your kind invitation for dinner on Tuesday, May the fifth, I now find that we cannot be there after all.

Mr. Jennings has just been called to Chicago on business; and although he tried very hard to postpone the trip until after the fifth, he was unable to do so.

We had been looking forward with great pleasure to seeing you and Dr. Benton; and we both feel very badly about this unexpected development. We hope you understand. and that you will not be inconvenienced.

Sincerely yours,
Susan Jennings

NOTE TO AN INTIMATE FRIEND RECALLING A DINNER INVITATION

Ruth, dear:

The dinner for Thursday, October the second, is off! Anita has the measles—of all things!—and it looks as though I'll have to suspend all plans for entertaining for the time being.

Anita isn't very ill; but she demands a great deal of attention and I'm with her most of the time. Then. too, of course. the measles are contagious—so this is certainly no time to have friends at the house!

I'm sure you and Bill will understand, Ruth—and ,that you will forgive this last—minute change in plans. I'll write you as soon as the Benton household is back to normal again, and we'll plan another date for dinner.

My love to you both!

Betty

NOTE TO AN INTIMATE FRIEND BREAKING A DINNER ENGAGEMENT

Dear Betty:

I'm so disappointed, I could cry! You know how I've been looking forward to your dinner next Thursday; and now, at almost the last moment, I find we can't make it after all.

As usual, Bill's been called out of town just when it's most inconvenient for us. He tried to postpone the trip for a few days, but couldn't do it. So here I am all alone again, Betty . . . with Bill on his way to Chicago . . . and both of us sorry as can be to break a dinner engagement with you at the last moment. I can't say I'd blame you if you stopped inviting us completely!

But you know it isn't our fault, darling. There's nothing we'd rather do than spend an evening with you and Tom. And we especially hate to miss those Nassau pictures! Will you let us come some evening and see them after Tom gets back?

Affectionately yours,
Ruth

A hostess who receives a note like the above should decide whether or not she wants her friend to come by herself. If she would rather not have an odd woman guest at the table, it's best not to answer the note at all; it doesn't actually require an acknowledgment. But if she wants her friend to come even without her husband. she telephones or writes at once, depending upon how much time remains. If there's no time for further correspondence, she calls and says in effect: "Never mind if Bill's out of town! Come to my dinner party anyway! I'm counting on you. . . ." Otherwise she writes a note somewhat along the lines of the following:

Dear Ruth:

Too bad Bill had to go out of town again so soon! He's practically commuting between New York and Chicago these days, isn't he?

But why don't you come to my dinner anyway, Ruth? I know it won't be nearly as much fun for you without Bill; but I think I can promise you a good time. The Norths and the Prestons will be here, and I know you always enjoy being with them. The Norths practically pass your house on the way home, and I'm sure they'll be glad to drop you off.

So come on, Ruth—and see those Nassau pictures I've been bragging about! Then we'll show them again some evening after Bill gets back, and he can see them too.

Remember—it's Thursday, October the second, at seven o'clock. Tom and I are looking forward to seeing you, so don't disappoint us!

Yours affectionately,
Betty

❑ ❑ ❑ ❑ ❑

Chapter III

LUNCHEON AND SUPPER INVITATIONS AND ACKNOWLEDGMENTS

Luncheons and suppers are, by their very nature, gay and light-hearted-the informal, and often impromptu, gathering of friends for a good time. They represent a less serious type of entertaining than dinners; and are for the most part quite simple and unpretentious in character.

Invitations for such functions are informal, too. More often than not they are just telephoned; or they are given casually, without previous plan, when friends chance to meet. Any written invitations are in the form of friendly little notes. Formal third-person invitations are rarely used for either a luncheon or supper; and then , only when it's a large, elaborate affair planned for some special purpose or to honor some special guest.

For example, a large and ceremonious luncheon is sometimes given, at home or at a hotel, to announce an engagement . . . to celebrate a wedding anniversary to present a debutante daughter . . . or for some similar purpose. Such socially important luncheons warrant the dignity and formality of engraved invitations. They are sent out two or three weeks in advance, and closely follow the phraseology of a dinner invitation:

Dr. and Mrs. Thomas Matthew Benton
request the pleasure of
Mr. and Mrs. Frank North's
company at luncheon
in honor of their daughter
Miss Anita Benton
on Saturday, May the third

at one o'clock
250 Park Avenue

Please respond

The person who receives such an invitation should answer at once with a definite acceptance or regret, following, the same formal wording as the invitation.

Another type of luncheon for which formal invitations are sometimes issued is the luncheon preceding an important sporting event such as a tennis match or football game. As only half a dozen people at the most are ordinarily invited to such a luncheon, invitations are rarely, if ever, engraved. They are carefully written by hand following the decorative spacing and arrangement of engraved formal invitations.

Mr. and Mrs. Robert G. Scully
request the pleasure of your company
at luncheon
Saturday, the eighteenth of August
at one o'clock
at the Pickwick Club
before the tennis finals at Lynn Field

Please send reply to
10 Lake Drive

The above invitation includes the tennis match following luncheon, the host and hostess assuming responsibility for the tickets. Therefore an acceptance or regret should be written and mailed at once, so that other disposition can be made of the tickets if you are unable to accept the invitation. (Do not **telephone** your reply to a formal invitation unless you have been out of town and return too late to write... in which case you should explain the circumstances to the hostess.)

As a rule, luncheons are not given jointly by a husband and wife, except for special occasions like the above. Most men cannot attend social functions in the middle of the day;

and luncheons are therefore generally planned for women alone, and invitations are issued in the name of the hostess alone. The name of the host never appears unless he is to be present at the luncheon and other men are to be invited as guests.

When a luncheon is given for a group of women—even a large, formal luncheon at a club or hotel—the invitations may be in the form of personal notes written by the hostess to her guests. But some women prefer formality even in their invitations, as they feel it gives more social significance to the occasion. Following is the standard form for an elaborate luncheon. It may be engraved for a large number of guests; but should be handwritten if only six or eight guests are invited.

Mrs. Thomas Matthew Benton
requests the pleasure of
your company at luncheon
on Friday, November the seventh
at one o'clock
250 Park Avenue

Please respond

Acceptance

Mrs. Wayne R. Pratt
accepts with pleasure
Mrs. Thomas M. Benton's
invitation for luncheon
on Friday, November the seventh
at one o'clock

Regret

Mrs. Wayne R. Pratt
regrets that a previous engagement
prevents her from accepting
Mrs. Thomas M. Benton's
invitation for luncheon
on Friday, November the seventh

It is not socially correct to write a personal note of explanation when declining a formal invitation. The regret should be as formal as the invitation itself, in the same wording and spacing. However, it is a courteous and friendly gesture to write a personal note to the hostess a week or so following the luncheon, to say how sorry you were to have missed it. This note would not be **instead** of the formal response, but in **addition to** it. It's one of those "letters-that-don't-need-to-be-written" which we discussed in an earlier chapter . . . letters that people do not expect, and are therefore especially delighted to receive.

When a luncheon is given to present a celebrity a new bride, or an out-of-town guest to a group of friends, that fact should be clearly specified in the invitation. If it's a personal note, as it's very likely to be, it should be brief and to the point:

Dear Mrs. Pratt:

Miss Marta Lang, the portrait painter, is visiting me this week and I am inviting a few friends to meet her. I am giving a luncheon on Thursday, September the third, at one o'clock; and I do hope you can come.

Miss Lang is a most charming and fascinating person, and I know you'll enjoy her company as much as she will enjoy yours. So please write and say you'll be here!

Cordially yours,
Elizabeth K. Bentan

If it's a formal invitation instead of a personal note, the phrase "To meet Miss Marta Lang" is used as the **first** or **last** line of the invitation:

To meet Miss Marta Lang
Mrs. Thomas Matthew Benton
requests the pleasure of

Mrs. Wayne R. Pratt's
company at luncheon
on Thursday, September the third
at one o'clock
250 Park Avenue

Please respond

or

Mrs. Thomas Matthew Benton
requests the pleasure of
your company at luncheon
on Thursday, September the third
at one o'clock
to meet Miss Marta Lang
250 Park Avenue

Whether an invitation specifically calls for a response or not, send an acceptance or regret promptly. It's difficult and inconvenient for a hostess not to know how many guests to expect. The reply to a personal note is, of course, a personal note:

Dear Mrs. Benton:

I'm delighted by your invitation to luncheon on Tbursday, September the third at one o'clock-to meet Miss Marta Lang.

I know Miss Lang's work and have long admired it; and I welcome this opportunity to make her personal acquaintance. Thank you for asking me!

Very sincerely yours,
Eleanor Pratt

The reply to a formal invitation can be only a formal acceptance or regret. A personal note or a telephone message may accomplish the same purpose, but does not do it properly from a social standpoint.

Acceptance

Mrs. Wayne R. Pratt
accepts with pleasure
Mrs. Thomas M. Benton's invitation to luncheon
on Thursday, September the third
at one o'clock
to meet Miss Marta Lang

Regret

Mrs. Wayne R. Pratt
regrets that she is unable to accept
Mrs. Thomas M. Benton's
kind invitation to luncheon
on Thursday, September the third
at one o'clock
to meet Miss Marta Lang
owing to a previous engagement

Sometimes a large and elaborate luncheon is given by two or more women. The invitations are usually engraved, and the names of all the women appear on it. For example:

Mrs. Carl Whitney
Mrs. Robert G. Scully
Mrs.Thomas Matthew Benton
request the pleasure of
your company at luncheon
on Wednesday, April the second
at half past one o'clock
The Savoy Plaza

Please reply to
Mrs. Thomas M. Benton
250 Park Avenue

Your reply to the above invitation should list **all** the names of the hostesses, exactly as in the invitation. But the envelope should be addressed only to the person whose name and address are indicated in the lower left corner. If no name and address are given, the envelope should be addressed to **all** the hostesses and sent to the hotel, as it can be assumed that arrangements have been made to receive them there.

INVITATIONS FOR SIMPLE INFORMAL LUNCHEONS

Up to this point we have been discussing formal ceremonious luncheons . . . elaborate social affairs that are sometimes given by husband and wife jointly, but are for the most part planned **by** women, **for** women . . . and usually for some very special occasion.

But far more familiar to most of us are the gay, informal luncheons that are planned for no other purpose than to enjoy the company of a few congenial, well-chosen friends. For most such luncheons, a telephone call is more likely than not to be the only invitation. But there are many who prefer writing personal notes of invitation, looking upon it as a somewhat more gracious custom.

The typical informal luncheon invitation is a brief note giving the time, the place and usually—but not necessarily—the reason for the luncheon.

Dear Ruth:

Will you come to luncheon on Friday, May the fifth. at one o'clock?

My niece, Doris Femell, is visiting us, and I think you will enjoy meeting her. She is a charming, witty girl, and very good company!

Laura Winston and Susan Jennings will be here, and perhaps we can play a little bridge after luncheon. Do say you'll come!

Affectionately yours,
Betty

Acceptance

Dear Betty:

How very nice to receive your invitation for luncheon on Friday, May the fifth! I'll be there promptly at one.

I'm looking forward to meeting your niece; she sounds fascinating. But most of all, Betty. I'm looking forward to seeing **you**! It's been a long time since I had that pleasure.

As ever,
Ruth

Regret

Dear Betty:

I can't think of anything I'd enjoy more than coming to your luncheon on Friday, May the fifth, and meeting your charming niece.

But darling, I **can't!** Friday's the day my sister is flying to Paris, and I promised to see her off. I'm due at the airport at one-thirty. She'll be expecting me, and I cannot disappoint her.

But thanks so much for asking me, Betty. I'm certainly sorry to miss your luncheon, and to miss meeting Miss Fernell.

Fondly,
Ruth

The response to a luncheon invitation should, of course be a definite acceptance or regret. But occasionally a hostess familiar with a friend's plans and eager to have that friend attend her luncheon, writes as follows:

> I know you are planning to be in Chicago on the tenth; but if you can possibly get back in time, will you come to my luncheon in honor of Kay Bolton, the writer?

In that case, the person who receives the invitation may answer in kind, giving neither a definite acceptance nor regret, but promising to come if she can:

> I'll try my best to be back by the tenth, as I'd like very much to come to your luncheon and meet Kay Bolton. But please don't count on it, as I wouldn't like to disappoint you.

If she returns in time—even if it's the very morning of the luncheon—she should telephone and say, in effect:

"Well, I made it! I'm home and I'm coming to lunch* today!"

If she does **not** get home in time, she should telephone or write immediately upon her return to say she was looking forward to the luncheon and was very sorry to have missed it.

INVITING SOMEONE YOU DO NOT KNOW

An ordinary note of invitation to; someone you know well is comparatively easy to write. But not all invitations are to intimate friends. Sometimes it's necessary to invite people you do not know well . . . perhaps do not know at all. Such letters are considerably more difficult to write.

The most important thing to bear in mind when inviting a stranger to luncheon (or to any other social affair) is that you must **explain the reason** for the invitation. Be sure it's a real reason, a **legitimate** reason, otherwise your invitation may seem offensive and in poor taste. It's important also to make your luncheon sound as though it will be interesting and enjoyable. Most people have busy social lives of their own, and do not like to accept invitations from strangers unless they know **why**, and can be reasonably sure they'll enjoy themselves if they accept.

---

* *The word "luncheon" is used in writing, and especially in invitations. The word "lunch" is more familiarly used in conversation. "Luncheon" has a somewhat more social implication, but it is rarely if ever* ***spoken.***

Dear Mrs. Johnson:

If you have no other plans for Wednesday, April the sixth, will you come to a little informal luncheon here at my home?

My Richard and your Larry have been roommates at Andover for so long that it's about time their mothers got to know each other—don't you think so?

I have asked two friends whom I think you will like; and perhaps we can play some bridge in the afternoon.

Luncheon is at one, and I'll expect you at that time unless I hear from you to the contrary.

Cordially yours,
Elizabeth K. Benton

If you receive a luncheon invitation like the above, and plan to accept it, you may reply or not as you prefer. An acknowledgment is not actually required, as your appearance on the day of the luncheon is expected if you do not send regrets within a day or two. However, a note like the following paves the way for a more friendly and cordial relationship:

Dear Mrs. Benton:

I'll be delighted to come to your luncheon on Wednesday, April the sixth, at one o'clock.

Larry has often spoken to me of Richard, and has told me how very much he enjoys having him for a roommate. Although I have never met Richard, I feel as though I know him from hearing so much about him.

I assure you it will be a very great pleasure indeed to meet Richard's mother! Thank you so much for asking me.

Sincerely yours,
Mildred Johnson

If you receive an invitation from someone you don't

know, and you cannot accept it, be sure that your reply is very carefully and very tactfully worded. For it would be most unkind to give the impression that you do not want to accept an invitation so graciously extended.

Dear Mrs. Benton:

I have heard so much about Richard from Larry that I almost feel as though I know him. I would certainly enjoy meeting his mother!

But unfortunately I expect guests myself on Wodnesday, the sixth of April; and therefore cannot accept your invitation for luncheon on that day.

It was thoughtful of you to invite me, and I am extremely sorry I cannot accept. I do hope you will ask me again some time!

Sincerely yours,
Mildred Johnson

However disappointed the hostess may be to receive a note like the above, she cannot feel hurt or resentful. For it is a gracious and friendly note, expressing sincere regret, and it gives a real excuse for not coming. In other words it does not slam the door shut...as **this** note does:

Dear Mrs. Benton:

I'm sorry I cannot accept your invitation for luncheon on Wednesday, April sixth, as I have other plans for that day.

Sincerely yours,
Mildred Johnson

Surely a cold, curt note like that leaves no further possibility of friendly overtures! It stamps the writer as rude and ill-mannered . . . and totally lacking in the social graces.

SUPPER INVITATIONS

Supper parties are the most **informal** of all types of

entertaining. Guests are generally intimate friends or members of the family; and invitations are almost always telephoned.

"How about you and Ted coming to supper next Tuesday night?" is the way supper guests are most likely to be invited. Or "We're having a buffet supper Sunday night. Can you and Bill come?"

A written note of invitation should be on about the same general level. If you customarily say to a friend. "How about supper Tuesday night?" —Don't suddenly become -stilted in your letter and write, "May we have the pleasure of entertaining you at supper next Tuesday evening?" Formal language doesn't go with simple supper informality. **Write it as you would say it**.

Dear Ann:

We're having a buffet supper Sunday night, June the fourth—and of course we want you and Bob!

Come at six, if you can. We'll have supper early and play some bridge afterwards. The Clarks and the Prestons will be here. and. I know you always enjoy their company.

We'll be expecting you on the fourth, so don't disappoint us!

With love,
Marjorie

No response to the above is necessary unless you like to be especially courteous and considerate. In that case, you write a note (always provided there is time, of course!) telling your hostess you'll be there. Ordinarily your presence at the supper party is all the acknowledgment necessary. But if you **cannot** attend the party, you must reply—and promptly.

Dear Marjorie:

I'm so sorry we can't come to your buffet supper Sunday

night! Bob's mother is ill, and we're going to Philadelphia this week end to see her.

Thanks for asking us. Marjorie. We certainly hate to miss any of your parties . . . they're always such fun!

Affectionately,
Ann

Guests do not ordinarily expect to meet strangers at an intimate supper party. Therefore if you are inviting someone outside your usual circle of friends and acquaintances, it's a good idea to explain about the details beforehand in your note of invitation:

Dear Margaret:

Do you remember Helen Foster, the girl who used to wear such funny hats at high school? Well, guess what! She's Ellen Fontaine now—the well-known fashion designer!

I told her about the work you are doing. and she is extremely interested. She wants to know more about your fashion-chart idea. I'm giving a buffet supper for her here at my apartment on Tuesday, May the tenth, and I'd like you to come. Then you can tell her about your work directly.

Supper is at seven o'clock. Ann and Bob will be here, and the Carters are coming in later. Do try and make it, Margaret! I think I can promise you an interesting evening.

Yours affectionately,

Eileen

Dear Eileen:

Imagine the famous Ellen Fontaine turning out to be that madcap Helen Foster we knew at high school! I can hardly believe it.

It will be very interesting to meet her again after all these years. And I just can't tell you how delighted I am at the chance to discuss my fashion charts with her!

I'm looking forward to Tuesday, May tenth, with great pleasure. Thanks for asking me, Eileen—I'm sure it will be a fascinating evening!

Affectionately yours,
Margaret

An invitation to share an evening with strangers is not always appealing to those who receive it. Consequently it should be made to **sound** interesting and worth while. In other words, the, invitation should "sell" the idea of accepting the invitation-should give a real reason for accepting it, and for looking forward to the occasion with pleasure and anticipation.

Dear Susan:

I know you are interested in old china and glassware, so I'm sure you'll be interested in the Bartons! They are coming here to supper next Sunday night. October the twelfth, and we'd like you and Walter to come, too.

The Bartons are that very charming couple we met in Montreal last summer. They have a wonderful collection of old china and glassware, and I understand that Mrs. Barton is quite an authority on English china. I'm sure you and Walter will thoroughly enjoy an evening in their company.

We're planning supper at six, that will give us a nice long evening to talk. If I don't hear from you before then, I'll be expecting you on the, twelfth!

Affectionately yours,
Laura

It is not easy to turn down an invitation so cordially and personally extended. The hostess who invites congenial people and plans an evening for their special enjoyment—and who goes to the trouble of writing notes to "sell" the evening to her guests—**should not be turned down unless absolutely necessary**. When an evening is so obviously planned for certain people, those people should make every effort to accept-even though it may mean a change in previous plans for the evening. If such plans cannot be changed, and the invitation cannot therefore be accepted, the hostess should be, notified immediately. It is then up to her either to proceed according to plan, or to postpone the supper until the people she wants can be there.

Dear Laura:

We would **love** to come to your supper on Sunday, the twelfth, and meet the Bartons. But that's the night Walter's brother is arriving from England, and he is expecting us to meet him at the airport and drive him home.

If it were anything else, Laura, we'd just change our plans and come. You know that, I'm sure. But we haven't seen Paul in nearly a year, and Walteris practically counting the hours to his arrival! We couldn't possibly disappoint him when we know he'll be expecting to see us as he steps off the plane. He is scheduled to arrive at six-fifteen., and as we are driving him out to Westchester, we couldn't get to your party until much too late.

We're **most** sorry to miss the opportunity of meeting the Bartons! Walter and I would have enjoyed so very much talking with them about old English china. But perhaps we'll have that pleasure at some future time.

You were sweet to ask us, Laura, and we appreciate it. Our very best to you and Jim!

With love,
Susan

Occasionally a supper of more elaborate and ceremo. aious proportions than the usual intimate type for friends is given for some special purpose. For example, instead of the elaborate formality of a dinner **preceding** the theater or opera (for a group of people who are to be entertained for one reason or another)—a supper is given **following** it. This is not, as a rule, the popular buffet supper, but a more impressive "sit down" affair. Nevertheless, invitations are still in the form of friendly, informal notes.

Dear Mrs. North:

We have eight tickets for the opening of the new Moss Hart show on Wednesday, September third. We are asking a group of friends to join us at the theater and come back with us later for a little supper party at the house. Dr. Benton and I hope that you and Mr. North have no previous engagement, and can join us for the evening.

We are meeting in the lobby of the Globe Theater at eight-fifteen. Please let us know if you **cannot** come; otherwise we will expect to see you there.

Cordially yours,
Elizabeth K. Benton

Acceptance

Even when an invitation specifically says to answer only if you cannot come, it is more gracious to send a note of acceptance.

Dear Mrs. Benton:

How very kind of you and Dr. Benton to include us in your theater and supper party for Wednesday, September third! We'll be delighted to come, and will be in the lobby of the Globe Theater at eight-fifteen.

It sounds like a wonderful evening, and we are looking forward to it with great pleasure. Thank you for asking us!

Cordially yours,
Alice North

Regret

Dear Mrs. Benton:

It is with the greatest reluctance that I must write and tell you we cannot accept your most generous invitation for

Wednesday. September third, for the Moss flart opening and your supper party afterwards.

. We are expecting friends from Canada; and as they will be here for that one evening only, we cannot leave them on their own.

Thank you very much for asking us. Mr. North and I sincerely regret missing such a marvelous party as yours promises to be!

Sincerely yours,
Alice North

❏❏❏❏❏

Chapter IV

PARTY INVITATIONS AND ACKNOWLEDGMENTS

The invitations you send out for your simple informal parties at home may be as original and "different" as you wish. It is not necessary to conform to any special wording or style. Birthday invitations may be in the form of amusing jingles. Shower invitations may be in the form of tiny, umbrella-shaped cards, if that appeals to your fancy. Invitations for holiday parties—such as Easter, Christmas, New Year—may be whatever is cleverly in keeping with the occasion.

But there are certain generalities of good taste that apply to **all** invitations. And there are certain basic "unwritten laws" of good hospitality that everyone should know about.

In the first place, no matter how informal the party may be, invitations should be sent out—or telephoned at least one week in advance. Obviously this doesn't apply to unplanned, impromptu parties for which no regular invitations are issued. It applies to the parties you plan ahead of time...and to which guests should be invited far enough in advance to make it **convenient for them to accept**. In these busy days it's definitely bad form to telephone or write even intimate friends just a day or two ahead of a party; for few people can accept such last-minute invitations without a hurried, last-minute change of plans—often at considerable inconvenience to others as well as themselves.

So if you like your friends and want to keep them, invite them as informally as you like . . . but **invite them well ahead of time**. And once you have arranged a party and invited your guests, don't make any sudden last minute change in plans unless absolutely necessary. To inconvenience half a dozen or more people for your own convenience is basically bad manners; and something not even a close friend soon forgets.

The second "unwritten law" of hospitality is to **choose your guests carefully**. Always try to invite people who are congenial and have something in common, and can therefore be reasonably expected to enjoy one another's company. Don't, for example, invite experts and beginners to the same bridge party. Don't invite two people you know dislike each other, or who are for one reason or another uncomfortable or unhappy in each other's company.

The keynote of good manners is **consideration for others.** That also is the keynote of good hospitality.

Don't invite a busy doctor on an evening when he has late office hours. Find out when he does **not** have regular hours, and plan your party for that evening.

Don't invite people who never drink to a cocktail party, nor people who do not enjoy cards to a card party.

Even the most simple, informal party should be planned for the enjoyment of the guests. If the people you invite are the kind who enjoy good conversation, and would rather sit around and talk than do anything else—don't try to foist charades or home movies on them! They'll have a much better time just talking.

So if yo want to be sure that your invitations are always received with pleasure and appreciation: (1) Plan your parties to suit the people you expect to invite. (2) Invite only those you know to be congenial. (3) Get your invitations out early! Give your guests the pleasure of looking forward to your party, instead of the inconvenience of scrambling about at the last minute trying to "make it."

CARD PARTY INVITATIONS

If you have friends who like to play bridge, canasta, or

gin rummy, one of the simplest and most enjoyable ways to entertain them is by means of a card party. Invitations are either by telephone or by informal note. Many hostesses prefer to telephone their bridge invitations, as this provides an immediate acceptance or regret from each guest, and tables can be arranged accordingly. However, notes of invitation are a shade more gracious. and somehow seem to give greater social significance to the occasion. If they are sent out well enough in advance and answered promptly, the hostess will have time to fill in, if necessary, and arrange the right number of players for each table.

Dear Ruth:

How would you and Bill like to play bridge on Friday evening, March the fourth? The Prestons and the Clarks are coming, and as you know, they're excellent players.

I hope you and Bill have no other plans for that evening, and that you can come. We're starting at about eight-thirty. Do try and make it, Ruth—we're looking forward to seeing you!

Affectionately yours,
Betty

An invitation calls only for an acceptance or regretnot for a long, chatty letter giving the local gossip and the family news. So answer as follows—briefly and to the point.

Dear Betty:

Bill and I haven't had a really good game of bridge in months, and we're delighted to come to your party on Friday, March the fourth.

We enjoyed the Clarks and Prestons very much the last time we met them at your house; and we're glad of this opportunity to see them again. I just hope Bill and I can hold up our end of the game—we're rather out of practice!

Thanks for asking us, Betty. We'll be there promptly at eight-thirty.

Affectionately yours,
Ruth

It's always better not to accept an invitation at all, than to accept it and be unable to go at the last minute. This is especially true of bridge invitations; for if you are expected and you fail to put in an appearance others are left out of the game. So if there's a possibility you may not be able to keep the engagement, say so frankly in a note of regret:

Dear Betty:

I wish I could accept your very tempting invitation to play bridge on Friday, March the fourth-but I hesitate to do so.

Bill has one of his usual deadlines to meet. He has been working night after night until ten or eleven o'clock; and although he says he may be through by the fourth, there's a very good chance that he **won't** be.

I wouldn't like to say "yes," Betty—and then find at the last minute that we can't come. So count us out this time; but many thanks for including us, and I hope you'll ask us soon again!

Affectionately,
Ruth

Many women like to entertain their friends at afternoon card parties; and frequently such parties are preceded by a luncheon. If it's a simple, informal party at home, the invitations are extended by telephone or personal note. But if it's a large bridge luncheon at a restaurant or hotel - perhaps to announce an engagement, or to honor a special guest—engraved invitations are usually sent out.

FOR AN INFORMAL BRIDGE LUNCHEON

Dear Marcia:

I understand you've been taking bridge lessons recently.

Well, here's your chance to show us what an expert you've become!

I'm having a group of friends here for luncheon and bridge next Tuesday, June the eighth. Can you come at one o'clock, and stay for most of the-afternoon?

Betty and Susan will be here, and I know they'll be disappointed if you can't come. But I'll be even **more** disappointed—it's such a long time since I've seen you! So please try your best to make it.

Affectionately yours,
Janet

FOR A FORMAL BRIDGE LUNCHEON

When a mother and daughter entertain at an afternoon party, the names of both appear on the invitation:

Mrs. Thomas Matthew Benton
Miss Anita Benton
request the pleasure of your company
at luncheon
Thursday. the twentieth of September
at one o'clock
The Hampshire House

Please reply to — Bridge
250 Park Avenue

FOR AN INFORMAL COCKTAIL PARTY

Dear Ruth:

We're having some friends in for cocktails on Friday, June the eighth, from four to six. Can you and Bill come?

Tom and I are looking forward to seeing you, so don't disappoint us!

Cordially yours,
Betty

FOR A FORMAL COCKTAIL PARTY

When invitations are issued for a cocktail party, the exact time of arrival and departure should be givenotherwise guests may stay too long and interfere with plans for the evening.

Dr. and Mrs. Thomas Matthew Benton
At Home
Friday, June the eighth
from four until six o'clock
250 Park Avenue

Cocktails

FOR AN INFORMAL TEA PARTY

A simple informal tea party at home is still one of the most gracious and charming ways of entertaining a group of favorite friends and interesting acquaintances. It is also a pleasant way for a bride who does not want to undertake elaborate luncheons or dinners to repay the hospitality of her friends.

A tea or "at home" is a type of reception, and is more strictly **social** in character than other forms of afternoon entertaining. Therefore even a quite small and informal tea party calls for **written** invitations. It's not considered good form to telephone your invitations for this type of party.

Dear Mrs. North:

I have asked some friends to come for tea on Tuesday, April the eighth, at four o'clock. Will you join us?

I know you have just returned from Bermuda, but I hope you're not too busy to come. I'm looking forward to seeing you.

Cordially yours,
Elizabeth K. Benton

If some special entertaining is planned for the afternoon, to that fact should be mentioned. An invitation is always more likely to be accepted if a **good reason** for accepting is given!

Dear Mrs. North:

Some of your good friends and mine are coming for tea on Tuesday, April the eighth, at four o'clock. I hope you can join us.

Rosa Cantrell is one of the guests and she has promised to sing for us. And Mrs. Winston is planning to show her Samoan movies. So **do** come if you can—it promises to be a most interesting afternoon!

Cordially yours,
Elizabeth K. Benton

Acceptance

Dear Mrs. Benton:

It does indeed promise to be an interesting afternoon . . . and I'm delighted to accept your invitation for Tuesday, April the eighth, at four o'clock!

I have heard about Mrs. Winston's fascinating Samoan movies, and I am looking forward to seeing them. And of course it's always a great treat to hear Rosa Cantrell!

You were sweet to include me, and I'am very happy to come.

Cordially yours,
Alice North

Regret

Dear Mrs. Benton:

I just can't tell you how sorry I am that I cannot accept your invitation for tea on Tuesday, April the eighth!

I have a club meeting that afternoon', and although I'd

gladly forego it if I could, I have a special report to make and must be present.

Thanks so much for asking me. I certainly hate to miss such a marvelous afternoon!

Cordially yours,
Alice North

FORMAL TEA PARTIES

Teas, like luncheons and other afternoon parties, are generally given by women alone; but sometimes they are given by "Mr. and Mrs." jointly. Such teas are formal and ceremonious, as a rule, and are given for some special purpose like honoring an important guest, presenting a debutante daughter, or announcing an engagement. The invitations for such teas or receptions may be handwritten, but usually they are engraved—especially if the affair is away from home, at a club or hotel.

For a formal tea given at home by a mother and her debutante daughter, the invitations are written or engraved as follows:

Mrs. Thomas Mathew Benton
Miss Anita Benton
At Home
Friday afternoon, October fifth
from four until seven o'clock
250 Park Avenue

For a formal tea given by a mother and her debutante daughter **away** from home, in a hotel, the invitations are exactly the same as the above ... except that the name of the hotel is given instead of the home address. If a reply is requested, that fact is indicated in the lower left corner, and the address for the reply is given.

When **both** parents receive with a debutante daughter, the invitations are issued by them jointly ... and men as well as women are invited to the party. Instead of "Mrs. Thomas Matthew Benton" in the invitation above, the top line reads "Dr. and Mrs. Thomas Matthew Benton." The rest of the invitation remains the same.

Sometimes a large formal tea is given at a hotel by the parents of two debutantes who are friends. For an important social function of this kind, invitations are almost always engraved—and read as follows:

Dr. and Mrs. Thomas Matthew Benton
Mr. and Mrs. Walter Jennings
Miss Anita Benton
Miss Suzanne Jennings
At Home
Friday, November the seventeenth
from four until seven o'clock
The Savoy Plaza

When a tea or reception is given in honor of a distinguished guest—or "to meet" a well-known personality—that person's name should appear first-on the invitation.

To Meet
Miss Rosa Cantrell
Dr. and Mrs. Thomas Matthew Benton
request the pleasure of your company
Tuesday, the fourth of March
from four until seven o'clock
The Sert Room
Waldorf-Astoria

Please respond to
250 Park Avenue

Formal tea invitations should be sent out ten days to two weeks in advance. The customary phrase is "At Home"—which simply means a social gathering, or reception. If the purpose of the tea is to meet a celebrity, the phrase "request the pleasure of your company" is preferred.

All such invitations are answered as written—in the same third-person phraseology, and with the same formal spacing. As a rule, one accepts an "At Home" simply by attending it unless a reply is specifically requested. But if one cannot accept, a regret should be sent promptly. All the names that appear on the invitation should be repeated in the acknowledgment.' For example:

Mr. and Mrs. Frank North
regret that they are unable to accept
Dr. and Mrs. Thomas M. Benton's
Mr. and Mrs. Walter Jennings'
Miss Anita Benton's
Miss Suzanne Jennings'
kind invitation for
Friday, November the seventeenth
owing to illness in the family

If no name and address for a reply are given on the invitation, it should be sent to the hotel where the reception is scheduled to be held. The envelope should be addressed to all the persons in whose names the invitations are issued.

GARDEN PARTY INVITATIONS

By "garden party" is generally meant a tea or reception held out-of-doors. If it's an important social function and formality is desired, the invitations may be engraved as follows:

Mr. and Mrs. Robert G. Scully
At Home
in the garden
Thursday, June the twenty-fifth
from three to six o'clock

But nowadays most garden parties are charmingly informal, and invitations are by friendly note:

Dear Joan:

Our garden has never been as lovely as it is now! We'd like our friends to see it, so we're having tea on the lawn next Thursday, June the twenty-fifth, from three to six o'clock.

We hope you and Ralph can come. You simply **must** see what a magnificent display of June roses we have this year!

Affectionately yours,
Martha

Acceptance

Dear Martha:

Ralph and I will be delighted to come to tea on the lawn Thursday, June twenty-fifth, at three o'clock.

Your garden is always lovely, but especially so this time of the year—and we're so glad to have an opportunity of seeing it. We're looking forward to it with great pleasure.

Affectionately yours,
Joan

Regret

Dear Martha:

How I wish I could come to your garden party next Thursday! But Ralph and I are going to Boston for a week, and we won't be back in time.

We both love your garden, especially this time of the year-and we're sorry to miss seeing it. But we're even more sorry to miss seeing you!

Thanks, Martha, for asking us ... I'll telephone you when we get back from Boston.

Affectionately yours.
Joan

INVITATIONS FOR HOUSE AND WEEK-END PARTIES

All invitations for house parties, whether for a week end or longer duration, should be by letter. There are many things the guest needs to know, and these should be included in the invitation.

For example, house guests must know the exact duration of the visit: when they are expected to arrive and when they are expected to leave. They should be given some idea of the activities planned, so that they will know what clothes and sports equipment to take with them. They should be told the best way to come, with marked road maps or timetables enclosed for their convenience.

A week-end visit is generally from. Friday or Saturday until the following Monday morning. Guests should be invited at least two weeks in advance, to give them time to make all necessary arrangements. If several members of a family are invited, they should all be mentioned specifically by name. The thoughtful hostess mentions what other guests have been invited, to avoid the possibility of bringing uncongenial people together for a week end.

Dear Jane:

I hope you and Fred haven't any plans for the week end of July twenty-fourth, as we'd like you to spend it with us at Far Acres. It's simply **beautiful** here now with everything in bloom!

I think we can promise Fred some good fishing this year. The trout are biting better than ever! So bring your fishing clothes; and be sure to bring your tennis things, too, because the Owens are coming and I'm sure you'll want to get out on the courts with them.

There's a very good train Friday night; I've marked it in red on the timetable. It gets you here about seventhirty, which is just in time for dinner. You can get a late train back

Sunday night, or there's an early express that Bob usually takes on Monday morning.

We hope nothing will prevent you from coming, as we're looking forward to your visit . . . and I know the Owens are looking forward to seeing you again, too. Be sure to let us know what train you are taking so that Bob can meet you at the station.

Affectionately yours,
Martha

Acceptance

Dear Martha:

Fred and I are counting the days to our week end with you at Far Acres! We are delighted that you have asked us; and we certainly won't let anything prevent us from coming.

We plan to take the five o'clock train on Friday night, July twenty-third, as you suggest. And we'll take the early express back to town on Monday morning.

Thanks so much for asking us. Martha! We're looking forward to two wonderful days with you and the Owens.

Affectionately yours,
Jane

Regret

Dear Martha:

How awful to have to turn down your very, very tempting invitation! I can't think of **anything** Fred and I would enjoy more right now than a week end at Far Acres. But I expect my mother just about that time—either on the twenty-third or twenty-fourth of July. She is stopping over on her way to Canada, and plans to spend a few days with us. Under the circumstances, we cannot make any plans for the week end.

But thanks so much for asking us, Martha! I know we're missing a marvelous time! Please remember us to the Owens, and tell them how sorry we are not to have been able to join them for the week end.

Affectionately,
Jane

People who own country houses often invite friends to house parties that may last anywhere from three days to three weeks. The invitation must give the exact date or expected arrival and departure. so that there can be no question about the duration of the visit. And like the week-end invitation it should indicate the best and most convenient way to come, the sports and activities planned, the clothes likely to be needed and so forth.

Dear Ruth:

As you know, Anita and I are at Shady Lawn for the summer. Tom is joining us here for two weeks at the end of August: and I'm planning a house party for that time so he'll be able to enjoy tennis and golf with the friends he likes best.

I'd like you and Bill to come, and to bring Marilyn along. We have a new boat this year, and I'm sure Marilyn and Anita will enjoy going out on the lake together.

Can you arrange to come to Shady Lawn on the sixteenth of August, and stay until the thirtieth? There's a very good train out of Grand Central at four-fifteen; it gets you here just in time for dinner. Try to take that train on Friday, the sixteenth, Ruth—and I'll see that someone meets you at the station. If Bill can't get away that early, there's a fast express Saturday morning. I've marked both trains on the timetable I'm enclosing.

I have asked the Norths and the Jennings to come; and Tom's brother may be here for a week or ten days. We should have lots of good bridge; they're all experts!

I'm looking forward to your visit, Ruth—and I know Tom will be delighted to have you and Bill here. So write and tell me you're coming!

With love,
Betty

Acceptance

Dear Betty:

Of course we'll come to your house party! We love Shady Lawn, and we love the Bentons . . . so how can we resist? In fact, Marilyn and Bill are so excited about it that they've talked of little else since your invitation arrived!

We plan to take the four-fifteen on Friday, August sixteenth, as you suggest. Bill may have to leave on the twenty-fifth; but Marilyn and I will stay until the thirtieth.

Thanks so much for asking us, Betty! We're looking forward to some wonderful swimming, fishing and all-around relaxing at Shady Lawn-but most of all. we're looking forward to being with you! We'll see you on the sixteenth.

With love to you and Anita,

Ruth

Regret

Dear Betty:

What a wonderful invitation—and how difficult for me to turn it down! But Bill can't get away in August this year; so we just can't come to your house party, much as we'd love to.

Bill tried to arrange things at the office, but it was out of the question. It seems that the campaign he is now working on must be ready by September first; and unless he stays right with it, he won't be able to complete it in time.

We certainly hate to miss a house party at Shady Lawn. Marilyn is practically **sick** about it! But I guess you'll have to count us out this year, Betty. . . .

Thanks for asking us, though—and we hope you, Tom and Anita thoroughly enjoy the rest of the summer!

With love,
Ruth

INVITATIONS FOR SHOWERS

The setting for a shower may be a luncheon, an afternoon tea, or an evening party . . . and the invitations may be telephoned, or they may be in the form of any attractive shower cards that appeal to you. Written invitations are simply informal notes giving the time, place, type of shower, and so forth.

Dear Miss White:

I am giving a linen shosver for Miss Mary Crawford on Saturday, April sixth, at four o'clock. I hope you can come, and stay for a buffet supper afterward.

This is a surprise for Mary, so please don't mention it to her if you see her before Saturday.

I have heard a great deal about you, from Mary's friends and I am looking forward to the pleasure of meeting you.

Sincerely yours,
Suzanne Jennings

Acceptance

Dear Miss Jennings:

I'll be delighted to come to the shower for Mary Crawford on Saturday, April sixth, at four o'clock—and to stay on for the buffet supper afterward. I'll bring something nice in linen for the bride-to-be.

Mary has spoken of you so many times that I almost feel as though I know you. I'm very glad of this opportunity to make your acquaintance.

Sincerely yours,
Helen White

Regret

Dear Miss Jennings:

I'm so sorry I must miss the shower you are giving for Mary Crawford on Saturday, April the sixth. I'll be out of town that week end.

However, I am sending a gift for Mary by mail. Will you-please put it with the other gifts for her?

Thanks for inviting me, and I do hope we shall have the pleasure of meeting some day. Mary has told me so many nice things about you!

Cordially yours,
Helen White

INVITATIONS FOR CHRISTENINGS

Most christenings are very informal affairs. Invitations are usually telephoned, or friends are asked when seen. But it is also correct to write brief friendly notes:

Dear Mrs. Whitney

Our new baby is to be christened at the Community Church next Sunday at four o'clock. We are planning to call him "Robert." Wouldn't you and Mr. Whitney like to come to the service?

Sincerely yours,
Derothy Evans

To an intimate friend, the note would naturally be less dignified and reserved:

Dear Kathleen:

That precious young son of ours is going to be christened next Sunday at four o'clock, at the Community Church. Come and see him make his first public appearance. He's simply **adorable,** Kathleen! We're planning to call him "Robert"—I hope you approve.

I'll be looking for you on Sunday—so be sure to come!

Affectionately yours,
Dorothy

Sometimes a business associate is invited to a child's christening and is unable to attend. When business interferes with the acceptance of any kind of invitation its gracious to imply you would have been **delighted** to accept otherwise.

Dear Mrs. Evans:

I am leaving for Los Angeles today on business. But it's with great reluctance that I do so, as I had hoped to attend 'your son's christening at the Community Church on Sunday.

I'm very sorry I won't be able to be there. Allow me, however, to wish-you great joy in your son; and to wish the young fellow himself a long and happy life.

Sincerely yours,
John T. McEiroy

There are usually two godmothers for a girl and one for a boy—two godfathers for a boy and one for a girl. They are chosen from among the relatives and intimate friends, and generally well before the baby's arrival. However, if someone living at a great distance is asked to be a godparent, a telegram is sent on the day of the child's birth—or very soon afterward.

It's a boy! Will you be godfather?

or

The baby arrived and it's a girl! We'd like you to be godmother.

A letter asking someone to be a godparent should be written with due regard for the seriousness of the occasion. It is no time to be flippant or facetious:

Dear Joan:

Our son is to be christened at the Community Church on Sunday, April the tenth, at four o'clock. We have decided to call him "Robert."

Joan, you and I were confirmed together; it would make me very happy if you would consent to be Robert's godmother. Peter Dawson and Kenneth Ayres will be the godfathers. I think you know them both.

We are planning to have a small dinner party at the house after the service, and we expect you to join us.

With affection,
Dorothy

The purpose of godparents is to provide "substitute parents" or protectors for a child, should it be left alone in the world. To be selected as a godparent is therefore somewhat of an honor—certainly an expression of trust and confidence in the person so selected. The request cannot very well be refused; on the contrary, it should be accepted with evident pleasure and pride, and with an appreciation of the responsibilities involved:

Dear Dorothy:

I'm proud and happy to be chosen as godmother for little Robert!

I warn you I shall take very seriously my share of the responsibility for your son's welfare, and shall keep a careful eye on the young man in the years ahead.

I'll be at your house about three o'clock on Sunday so that I can go to the church with you, and perhaps be of some help on the way.

Affectionately,
Joan

❐ ❐ ❐ ❐ ❐

Chapter V

DANCE INVITATIONS AND ACKNOWLEDGMENTS

THE days of large, colorful balls and receptions are over, but the dance as a social function remains as popular as ever.

The word "ball" is rarely used on invitations nowadays, except for a large public subscription dance or a charity affair. For ordinary social invitations, formal or informal, the word "dance" is used. The phrase "a small dance" frequently appears on formal invitations, regardless of the size of the function.

Invitations for formal dances are usually engraved, and are sent out from two to three weeks in advance. Following are the most familiar and acceptable forms:

Dr. and Mrs. Thomas Matthew
Benton request the pleasure of your company
at a small dance
Thursday, the eighth of November
at ten o'clock
The Savoy Plaza

Please reply to
250 Park Avenue

The fill-in type of invitation (with the guest's name written in by hand) is somewhat more personal, and for that reason many people prefer it. Instead of "at a small dance" in the body of the invitation, the word "Dancing" may be used in the lower right corner.

Dr. and Mrs. Thomas Matthew Benton
request the pleasure of
Mr. and Mrs. Frank North's
company on Thursday, the eighth of November
at ten o'clock
The Savoy Plaza

Please reply to Dancing
250 Park Avenue

The most formal and precise invitation of all is the "At Home" with "Dancing" in the lower left or right corner. It may be used whether the dance is for twenty or thirty people in a private house—or for several hundred people, with an entire floor of a large hotel engaged for the purpose:

Mr. and Mrs. Paul Preston
At Home
Tuesday, the third of April
at ten o'clock
The Drake

Kindly send reply to Dancing
20 Lake Drive

When a dance is given by two couples. the names of both should appear on the invitation. If a reply is requested, the name of the person to whom it should be sent is indicated:

Mr. and Mrs. John Arnold
Mr. and Mrs. Henry S. Schuyler
request the pleasure of your company
at a small dance
Friday, the fifth of November
at ten o'clock
The Lowell Country Club

Please address reply to
Mrs. John Arnold
10 Vedon Square

Dances are frequently given in honor of an important guest or someone who is to be especially honored. The name of that guest should always appear on the invitation. Either of the two following forms are correct and may be used:

Dr. and Mrs. Thomas Matthew Benton
request the pleasure of your company
at a dance in honor of
Miss Doris Fernell
Thursday, the eighth of November
at ten o'clock
The Savoy Plaza

or

To Meet
Miss Doris Fernell
Dr. and Mrs. Thomas Matthew Benton
request the pleasure of
Mr. and Mrs. William Forester's
company on Thursday, the eighth of November
at ten o'clock
The Savoy Plaza

Dancing

Masquerade and costume dances are based on the idea that people like to throw off conventional garb once in a while, and dress up to represent an entirely different character or personality than their own. Such dances are especially suitable for young people home from school for the holidays. Invitations are exactly like any formal dance invitations, except that "costume dance," "masquerade" or "fancy dress" appears somewhere on the invitation to show what kind of dance it is. Two examples follow:

Dr. and Mars. Thomas Matthew Benton
request the pleasure of your company
at a costume dance for their daughter

Miss Anita Benton
Thursday, the eighth of November
at ten o clock
The Savoy plaza

or

Dr. and Mrs. Thomas Matthew Benton
request the pleasure of your company
at a small dance
to be given at their home
on Thursday, the eighth of November
at ten o 'clock
250 Park Avenue

Please respond Fancy Dress

If a special kind of costume is to be worn—representing famous personalities of the past, characters from books, the dress of colonial times, and so forth—that fact should be indicated in the lower left corner of the invitation.

DEBUTANTE DANCES AND DINNER DANCES

The most popular form of invitation for a dance in honor of a debutante daughter is as follows:

Mr. and Mrs. Walter Jennings
request the pleasure of
Miss Anita Benton's
company at a dance in honor of their daughter
Miss Suzanne Jennings
Wednesday evening, October the seventh
at ten o'clock
One East Sixtieth Street

R.S.V.P.

The formal "At Home" is also correct for a debutante dance, with the name of the daughter at the top of the invitation with those of her parents:

Mr. and Mrs. Walter Jennings
Miss Suzanne Jennings
At Home
Wednesday, October the seventh
at ten o'clock
One East Sixtieth Street

Please respond Dancing

If the dance is held away from home, at a club or hotel, the following invitation is correct:

Mr. and Mrs. Walter Jennings
request the pleasure of your company
at a small dance in honor of their daughter
Miss Suzanne Jennings
on Wednesday, October the seventh
at ten o'clock
The Ambassador

A dinner dance is by far the favorite type of entertainment for a debutante daughter. Often two groups of guests are invited: one group for dinner and dancing, another for dancing only. In that case two separate sets of invitations are issued: regular dance invitations for those who are to come **after** dinner, and invitations like the following for those who are invited for both dinner and dancing:

Mr. and Mrs. Walter Jennings
request the pleasure of your company
at dinner
in honor of their daughter
Miss Suzanne Jennings
Wednesday, October the seventh
at eight o'clock
The Ambassador

Please reply to Dancing at ten
One East Sixtieth Street

or

Mr. and Mrs. Walter Jennings
request the pleasure of
Mr. and Mrs. James Winston's
company at a dinner dance for their daughter
Miss Suzanne Jennings
on Wednesday, October the seventh
at eight o'clock
The Ambassador

Please address reply to
One East Sixtieth Street

SUPPER DANCE INVITATIONS

Nowadays supper parties are frequently given to honor a special guest or a debutante daughter, or to introduce a new daughter-in-law. These dances are simple and unpretentious compared to the great "balls' of the past; but the same precise formality is maintained in the invitation. Following is the correct invitation for a debutantes formal supper dance at home:

Mr. and Mrs. Walter Jennings
Miss Suzanne Jennings
request the pleasure of your company
at a supper dance
Wednesday, October the seventh
at half past ten o'clock
One East Sixtieth Street

The favor of a reply
is requested

If the supper dance is held at a hotel, and is for the purpose of presenting a new daughter-in-law to one's friends, either of the following two invitations may be used:

To meet
Mrs. Arthur Blanchard
Mr. and Mrs. Floyd T. Blanchard
request the pleasure of your company
at a supper dance
on Tuesday, September the fifth
at ten o'clock
The St. Regis

R.s.v.p.
One University Place

or

Mr. and Mrs. Floyd T. Blanchard
request the pleasure of
Mr. and Mrs. Frederick Steele's
company at a supper dance in honor of
Mrs. Arthur Blanchard
on Tuesday, September the fifth
at ten o'clock
The St. Regis

Please send reply to
One University Place

Occasionally an afternoon tea with dancing is given for a debutante, or to introduce a son's bride. The invitation is generally a formal "At Home," with the name of the hostess and her guest of honor at the top:

Mrs. Floyd T. Blanchard
Mrs. Arthur Blanchard
At Home
on Tuesday, the fifth of September
from four until seven o'clock
The St. Regis

Dancing

HOW TO ACKNOWLEDGE FORMAL DANCE INVITATIONS

All formal invitations should be answered in formal, third-person phraseology. The acceptance or regret should be carefully handwritten on one's best white note paper, in the same arrangement as the invitation and following the same wording.

Acceptances

Mr. and Mrs. Frank North
accept with pleasure
Dr. and Mrs. Thomas M. Benton's
kind invitation to be present
for dancing
on Thursday, the eighth of November
at ten o'clock
at the Savoy Plaza

Mr. and Mrs. Philip Duell
accept with pleasure
Mr. and Mrs. John Arnold's
and Mr. and Mrs. Henry S. Sebuyler's
kind invitation for dancing
on Friday, the fifth of November
at ten o'clock
at the Lowell Country Club

Miss Anita Benton
accepts with pleasure
Mr. and Mrs. Walter Jennings'
invitation to a dance in honor of
Miss Suzanne Jennings
on Wednesday, October the seventh
at ten o'clock

Regrets

Mr. and Mrs. Frank North
regret that they are unable to accept
Dr. and Mrs. Thomas M. Benton's
kind invitation for dancing
on Thursday, the eighth of November
at ten o'clock
owing to a previous engagement

Mr. and Mrs. William Forster
regret that they will be unable to attend
Dr. and Mrs. Thomas M. Benton's
dance in honor of
Miss Doris Fernell
on Thursday, the eighth of November
as they will be out of town

Mr. and Mrs. Frank North
regret that owing to illness
they are unable to accept
Dr. and Mrs. Thomas M. Benton's
kind invitation to a costume dance
for their daughter
Miss Anita Benton
on Thursday, the eighth of November

Frequently a formal regret is followed up by a personal note a or so after the dance. This is not an obligation, but it's a courteous and thoughtful thing to do. If the dance was for a debutante or a special guest, it's a friendly gesture to send flowers a few days after the dance, with a brief note saying how sorry you were to miss it.

RECALL OR POSTPONEMENT OF FORMAL DANCE INVITATIONS

If an invitation must be recalled, it is always more polite to give the reason for it. A simple announcement like the following is usually sent out. It may be either printed on cards, or carefully written by hand on plain white note paper. As a rule, there is not enough time to have such announcements engraved.

Dr. and Mrs. Thomas Matthew Benton
regret that they are obliged to recall their invitations
for Thursday, the eighth of November
owing to the illness of their daughter

The postponement of a dance may be indefinite, or another date may be specified. For example:

Mr. and Mrs. Walter Jennings
regret that owing to illness in the family
their dance for Wednesday, October the seventh
is temporarily postponed

or

Mr. and Mrs. Walter Jennings
wish to announce
that the dinner dance in honor of their daughter
has been postponed until
Wednesday, October the twenty-first
at eight o'clock
The Ambassador

Please send reply to
One East Sixtieth Street

It is always best to repeat the hour and the place, even though they are the same as in the original invitation. If an invitation is merely postponed and not canceled, it isn't necessary to give a reason or make an explanation.

SUBSCRIPTION DANCES AND CHARITY BALLS

When a large dance is given by a club or association, and attendance is by paid subscription, a return card and envelope are usually enclosed. The return of the card with a check for tickets is the only acknowledgment required. No formal acceptance of the invitation need be written ... nor is a "regret" expected if you do not plan to attend.

Bear in mind that the word "ball" may be used only in invitations like the following—invitations to large public or semi-public affairs:

The Entertainment Committee of the Ferndale Club
requests the pleasure of your company
at a Ball
to be held at the club house
on Friday, the fifth of October
at ten o'clock
for the benefit of
The Community Hospital

Tickets five dollars

or

The pleasure of your company is requested
at the
Annual Masquerade Ball
of the Women's Advertising Club
to be held at the Marshland Hotel
on Tuesday, the fifteenth of November
at half past ten o'clock
for the benefit of
The Guild for the Blind

The subscription is three dollars
for each person

Frequently the invitations to a dance issued by a club list the names of the patrons or patronesses. If there are just a few names, they may appear on the face of the invitation, as shown below. But if there are many names, they should be listed separately on the inside or reverse side of the invitation. Occasionally the addresses of the patrons are also given when tickets are on sale at their homes.

The pleasure of your company is requested
at a Spring Dance
on Saturday evening, the second of May
at ten o'clock
The Wynnfield Cub

Patronesses

Mrs. Robert Bruce	Mrs. Charles Cort
Mrs. John T. Price	Mrs. Earle Higgens
Mrs. Arthur Hervey	Mrs. Charles Gordon

Please send reply to

Dance Committee	Tickets five dollars
The Wynnfield Club	for each person

Invitations to subscription dinner dances usually give the name of the person through whom reservations can be made. For example:

The Graduating Class of 1938
Hahnemann Medical College and Hospital
invites you to attend a
Dinner Dance
at
The Bellevue-Stratford
Wednesday, the fourth of October
at half past seven o!clock

Make reservations through

Miss Margaret Baker	Tickets five dollars
11 Rittenhouse Square	for each person

INVITATIONS FOR INFORMAL DANCES

Some people still cling to the custom of using visiting cards as informal invitations to dances, teas, musicales, even luncheon and supper parties. They simply scribble the few necessary words in a corner of the card—usually the lower left corner—and let it go at that!

We cannot approve this use of visiting cards for invitations. It's a careless and "sloppy" social habit, and should not be encouraged. Originally intended as a convenient substitute for engraved third-person forms, visiting card invitations have a curt and unflattering connotation. They sound **hurried**. They have neither the dignity of formal engraved invitations, nor the warmth and charmer friendly informal notes.

However, as some people still use visiting cards for invitations, and you will no doubt continue to receive them from time to time, you should know what kind of party they represent—and what kind of acknowledgment you are expected to write.

If you receive an invitation like one of, the following, you can expect a not-too-formal party, somewhat more important socially than a simple little supper or dance for intimate friends would be, but not important or elaborate enough to warrant engraved invitations.

These invitations should be answered at once whether a reply is requested or not, and they should be answered by personal note. It may be more convenient to write, "Delighted! Sunday at eight" on your own visiting card and send it to your hostess. And fundamentally, of course, that's no more incorrect than the invitation is. But it's so much more courteous to write a friendly note . . . just as it would have been more courteous to write a friendly **note of invitation** instead of sending a visiting card!

So whenever you receive a visiting card invitation, write a brief but cordial note in response. If it's an acceptance, write with evident pleasure; make it clear you are looking forward to the occasion:

Dear Mrs. Maitland:

What a pleasant surprise to receive your invitation for Tuesday, June 14th, at 10 o'clock! Dr. Benton and I will be **delighted** to come.

Mr. and Mrs. Frank Price

Buffet Supper — *R. S. V. P*
Sunday at Eight — 30 Lake Drive

Mr. and Mrs. Robert *Maidand*

Dancing at 10
Tues. June 14 — 400 Park Avenue

To Meet
Mrs. Joel Kane
Mr. George Warren

Wed. June 6
Bridge at 4 — Highbridge Road

May I add that we are looking forward with great pleasure to swing you and Mr. Maitland again!

Sincerely yours,
Elizabeth K. Benton

If you cannot accept the invitation, explain why in your note. If there is no real reason, if you just don't want to go, the easiest way out is to say you have another engagement but say it graciously and with apparent regret:

Dear Mrs. Maitland:

I'm so disappointed not to be able to accept your kind invitation for Tuesday, June 14th. We have, another engagement for that evening—one we cannot very well get out of.

Dr. Benton and I sincerely regret not being able to come, and we hope you understand and forgive us under the circumstances.

Cordially yours,
Elizabeth K. Benton

THE FRIENDLY NOTE OF INVITATION

When you plan a simple, informal dance to celebrate a birthday or anniversary, to entertain a son or daughter home from school, or perhaps merely to repay a group of friends for their hospitality to you—you invite your guests either by telephone or by note. It's always more desirable to write notes if you have the time. They may be as short as you like, but they should be **cordial**. Following are several examples for various types of small dances:

Dear Mrs. Brown:

Will you and Mr. Brown give us the pleasure of your company on Thursday, March eighth, at ten o'clock? We are planning a small, informal dance, and Dr. Benton and I should like very much indeed to have you join us.

We do hope you have made no other arrangements for the eighth, and that we can look forward to seeing you.

Sincerely yours,
Elizabeth K. Benton

Dear Ruth:

Next Friday, September the fifth, is Tom's birthday and I thought it would be pleasant to have some of his friends here to help him celebrate. Will you and Bill come? We'll have dancing from nine until midnight, and then cut the birthday cake!

Tom and I are both very eager to have you here. so don't disappoint us!

Affectionately yours.
Betty

Dear Suzanne:

Richard will be home for Thanksgiving next week. We are having some of his friends in for dancing on Friday evening, the twenty-third, and I hope you can come.

The dancing will be from nine-thirty to midnight. and we'll see that you get home safely. So **do** come!

Sincerely yours,
Elizabeth K. Benton

Dear Peter:

Mother has asked me to invite a few friends to a small, informal dance she is giving for me next Wednesday, April third, at nine o'clock.

Many people you know will be here-and I hope you can come, too.

Sincerely yours,
Anita Benton

Dear Julie:

If you meet a witch or a ghost on the way here Saturday night, October the sixteenth, don't be alarmed! They'll just be guests on their way to our masquerade.

I'd like you and your brother Bob to come. You can dress here if you like, or you can come all dressed and masked so that nobody recognizes you. I that's more fun!

Come at nine, Julie. There'll be dancing until eleven, and a buffet supper afterward. I hope that both you and Bob can make it.

With love,
Anita

It's entirely proper to write, "I'd like you and your brother to come" in an informal invitation. But do not address the envelope to "Miss Julie Clark and brother. That's distinctly bad form. A note written to one person should never be addressed in any way except to that one person.

Acceptances

Dear Mrs. Benton:

Mr. Brown and I will be delighted to come to your dance on Thursday, March the eighth, at ten o'clock. It was kind of you and Dr. Benton to think of us, and to include us among your guests.

We look forward with much pleasure to seeing you both again.

Cordially yours,
Millicent Brown

Dear Betty:

Of course we'll come and help Tom celebrate his birthday! It sounds like lots of fun.

Friday, September the fifth, at nine...it's a date! Bill and

I will be there promptly. And thanks so much for asking us!

Affectionately,
Ruth

Dear Mrs. Benton:

I'll be very glad to come for dancing on Friday evening, the twenty-third, at nine-thirty.

I think it was very kind of you to ask me!

Sincerely yours,
Suzanne Jennings'

Remember that even between good friends, notes of invitation and acknowledgment should be brief and to the point, Don't let yourself be tempted to write of other things.

Dear Anita:

I'm certainly glad you invited me to your dance on Wednesday, April third, at nine o'clock. I'd have hated to miss it!

Thanks for asking me. I'll sure be looking forward to April the third!

Sincerely yours,
Peter Whitney

Dear Anita:

What fun! Masquerades are my favorite kind of party, and I wouldn't miss yours for anything!

Bob and I will be there on Saturday, the sixteenth, at nine o'clock. We're coming all dressed and masked, and we **hope** you won't know who we are!

I'm so glad there'll be dancing, Nita. You know how I love it! Bob does, too—and he says to be sure and thank you for inviting him.

With love to you and your mother,

Julie

Regrets

Dear Mrs. Renteli:

It was very kind of you and Dr. Benton to invite us for Thursday. March the eighth—and we are extremely sorry that we cannot accept.

Mr. Brown must leave for Los Angeles on the seventh. He tried to postpone the trip for a few days, but was unable to do so.

But thank you so much for asking us, and we hope to have the pleasure of seeing you both soon.

Cordially yours,
Millicent Brown

Dear Betty:

It's not easy to say "no" to a party at your house—especially when it's to help Tom celebrate his birthday, but we just can't help ourselves! Bill invited some clients for dinner on Friday, the fifth, and I just don't see how we can get out of it gracefully.

Bill is as disappointed as I am. We certainly wish either **our** dinner or **your** dance were on another evening!

Please give our love and congratulations to Tom on his birthday, and tell him we're sorry as can be to miss his party. We'll have to come and pay our respects another time.

Thanks for asking us, Betty—and our sincere regrets!

Devotedly yours,
Ruth

Dear Mrs. Benton:

I'd love to come to your dance for Richard on Friday, the twenty-third, but mother and I are going to Baltimore for the week end to be with my sister. Both she and the baby have been ill.

Thanks for asking me, Mr. Benton I think it was very

sweet of you. I'm sure you must know how disappointed— I am not to be able to accept.

Sincerely yours,
Suzanne Jennings

Dear Anita:

Gosh, I'm sorry—but my cousin's being married on Wednesday, April the third, and we're all going to Scarsdale for the wedding. I sure wish the bride had picked some other day!

It was swell of you to invite me to your dance, and I hate to miss it. Please give my regrets to your mother, too.

I hope you'll give me the chance to say "yes" some other time, Anita.

Sincerely yours.
Peter Whitney

Dear Anita:

My mother and dad are celebrating their wedding anniversary on Saturday, October the sixteenth, and of course they expect Bob and me to be with them. Dad has tickets for the theater, and I think he has made a reservation for somewhere afterwards—but he won't tell us the details. He says it's a surprise.

Bob and I simply **hate** missing your masquerade-it sounds like such fun! And you know how we both love to dance! But it's just one of those things, Nita. . . We can't let mother and dad down.

I'll be thinking of you on the sixteenth, and wishing I were there. Bob says to be sure and thank you for asking him; he's as sorry to miss your party as I am.

With love,
Julie

ASKING AN INVITATION FOR A RELATIVE OR FRIEND

It is never permissible to ask for an invitation of any kind for yourself. Nor is it permissible to ask for a luncheon or dinner invitation for someone else. But if you are invited to an informal dance, and you have someone staying with you at the time—or you would like to take someone along whom you think your hostess would enjoying meeting—it's entirely proper to ask for an invitation.

Dear Mrs. Benton:

I know that you and Dr. Benton are interested in Indian folklore and legend. My nephew, Ralph Harris, who has just written a book about the Indians of New York State, is staying. with us—and I would like to bring him to your dance on Thursday, March the eighth. I think you will enjoy meeting him; and I know **he** will enjoy seeing, your unusual Indian collection.

May I bring him? I know he'll be delighted to receive your invitation. But if you feel you cannot invite another guest, please say so frankly and I'll understand.

Mr. Brown and I are looking forward with pleasure to the eighth!

Cordially yours,
Millicent Brown

Dear Betty:

Bill's brother has just arrived unexpectedly from California; and as he'll only be here a few days, we don't like to desert him even for an evening.

So may we bring him to your dance on the fifth? He's a most charming and congenial person, and I'm sure you and Tom will enjoy meeting him.

But if you'd rather not have an extra guest, Betty—Please say so! We'll get him a ticket for the theatre or something, and come help Tom celebrate his birthday anyway!

Affectionately yours,
Ruth

Dear Mrs. Benton:

I would love to come to your dance on Friday, the, twenty-third—but I have a house guest this week, and I can't very well leave her alone for the evening.

Her name is Janet Carey. She lives in Virginia and she is my roommate at school.

I know she would be very happy if you invited her by the dance, and I'd like very much to bring her. But if it would be inconvenient for you to have another guest, please tell me!

Thank you for inviting me, Mrs. Benton. I do hope you won't think I'm too presuming in asking to bring my friend.

Sincerely yours,
Suzanne Jennings

The hostess who receives such a note should reply at once, either extending a courteous invitation to the stranger, or explaining frankly why she cannot do so.

Dear Suzanne:

By all means bring Miss Carey with you to the dance on Friday, the twenty-third! I'll be delighted to have her.

Sincerely yours,
Elizabeth K. Benton

or

Dear Suzanne:

I would be very happy to include your friend among my guests for the twenty-third, but so **many** of Richard's friends are coming that I'm afraid there will be very little space for dancing as it is.

I hope you understand, and that you will give me the opportunity of meeting Miss Carey some other time.

Sincerely yours,
Elizabeth K. Benton

❑ ❑ ❑ ❑ ❑

Chapter VI

WEDDING INVITATIONS AND ANNOUNCEMENTS

IN the start of their social life together, a bride and groom naturally wants to be **correct**. They want their wedding. to be perfect in every detail, as traditionally beautiful and dignified as they can make it.

With all the many other things to plan and decide in connection with the ceremony and reception, it's nice to know that in the matter of invitations there need be no problem, no difficulty. Here at least it's easy for the bride and groom to make their choice, and to know that their choice is the right one. For whether a wedding is of great social importance or great simplicity, the forms are fixed by custom and long usage . . . and it's necessary only to select the particular invitation or announcement that suits the circumstances.

All the approved engraved forms for church and home weddings are given in this chapter, as well as suggestions for the simple, informal notes that are written by hand when the wedding is a very small and intimate one. But first, here is a general commentary on the etiquette of wedding invitations . . . answers to the questions people ask most frequently on the subject:

1. Everything about a wedding should be in quiet dignity and good taste, including the invitations and announcements. Only white paper of finest quality should be used, and it should be entirely without decoration—except, perhaps, for a family crest or coat of arms embossed without color. Gilt edges, borders, monograms, entwined initials are all in extremely bad taste.

2. Engraved invitations are traditional for all weddings. large and small. But if it's a very simple, informal wedding for just a few relatives, or a quiet wedding, due to a recent death in the family, invitations may be by personal note, or even by telephone. In this case, formal announcements are usually sent on the day of the wedding, or soon after, to everyone on the mailing list of both families.
3. Wedding invitations come in two sizes: **large** double sheets which fold once into the envelope, and **smaller** double sheets which slide into the envelope without folding. Both are correct. But it is **not** good form, to use cards or single sheets.
4. The engraving is always in black. The style of lettering depends on personal choice, and on the size of the invitation.
5. Wedding invitations and announcements are usually enclosed in two envelopes, although one may be used. When two are used, the inside envelope is left unsealed (should not be gummed). The invitation, reception card, and whatever other cards or enclosures are required, are placed in this inside envelope. Tissue, if provided by the stationer, is left in place to prevent smudging.

   Only the name or names of the persons being invited are written on the inside envelope. If Mr. and Mrs. John Malcolm Stewart and their two children are invited, the inside envelope reads:

   Mr. and Mrs. Stewart
(No given name)
Judy and Neal
(Children under 21)

   An adult son or daughter living at home should receive a separate invitation. The phrase "and family" should not be used, on the inside or outside envelope. Two adult sisters are addressed as "Misses Jean and Harriet

Stewart" on the outside envelope, "The Misses Stewart" on the inside envelope. Two adult sons are addressed as "Messrs (or "The Messrs.") Neal and Craig Stewart" with "Messrs. Stewart" on the inside envelope.

Even when several children are included on the inside envelope, the outside envelope is addressed to the parents only. Here, of course, the full name is used, initials should be avoided if possible. It is traditional for wedding invitations and announcements to be addressed by hand; and only black ink should he used.

Place the inside envelope into the outer one so that the name of the guest faces forward. Just insert it with its flap, or back, facing the raised flap of the outside envelope and it will be in the proper position. The use of two envelopes is not for formality only; the outside envelope protects the invitation and enclosures.

6. Start making your guest list well ahead of time; and be sure to order an adequate supply of invitations. It's better to have a few left over than to discover at the last moment that you forgot a distant cousin or an old school friend, and haven't another invitation to send. Relatives or friends in distant places, or in mourning, may be invited even though they are not expected to attend.
7. Wedding invitations should be mailed at least one month in advance; and as engraving takes time, be sure to see your stationer early. You will find it helpful to have the outside envelopes delivered a week or two ahead of time so that they can be addressed and ready to mail by the time the engraved invitations arrive.
8. Announcements should be ordered at the same time as the invitations, and should be similar in style and wording. They are mailed on the day of the wedding or **after** it, to those who did not receive invitations.
9. Invitations and announcements are issued by the bride's parents, even though she may not be living, at home.

If one parent is dead, the invitations are issued in the name of the remaining parent. If neither parent is living, the invitations are issued by the nearest relative (like a married brother and his wife) or by a guardian. In rare cases, when there are no relatives and no guardian, the invitations may be issued by an intimate friend-or the bride and groom may send them out in their own names. In the latter case, the bride's name comes first. When invitations or announcements are issued by someone other than the bride's parents, or a relative with the same name as her own, the bride's **full name** should be used to prevent confusion.

10. Parents who are separated may unite their names on the occasion of their daughter's wedding, if they so wish. Thus the invitations may be issued by "Mr. and Mrs. Frank B. Mitchell" even though "Mr." and "Mrs." have been living apart for many years. But if parents are legally divorced, and especially if one or the other has remarried, the invitations should be issued only in the name of the parent with whom the daughter has been living. If that parent has remarried, the invitations should be issued in the names of the parent and the new mate. It would be a glaring discourtesy to issue the invitations in the name of a parent alone, when that parent has remarried and the bride has been making her home with both. When a bride has lived part of the time with one parent and part of the time with the other, the invitations are usually issued in the name of her mother.*

11. The year is not necessary on wedding invitations, and is not ordinarily used. But if it is used, it should be written as spoken: "Nineteen hundred and sixty." The form, "One thousand. nine hundred and sixty" is an affectation and should be avoided.

---

* *Examples of invitations to meet special and unusual circumstances will be found on pages 118 to 127.*

12. The year **should** be given on wedding announcements—also the city or town in which the ceremony was held. This applies even after an elopement, and regardless of the time that has elapsed between the marriage and the announcement. But the name of the church or the house address where the ceremony was Performed is not necessary, though it is frequently given.

13 Numbers, names, street addresses, dates should all be spelled out in full on an engraved invitation or announcement. Numerals may be used only if an address is unusually long and would look clumsy and unattractive if spelled out on the invitation.

14 If necessary, the street address may be engraved under the name of the church.

15. The word "to" is used between the names of the bride and groom on announcements and on invitations to the ceremony. But the word "and" is grammatically necessary instead of "to" on invitations to a wedding breakfast or reception—because by that time the bride and groom are already man **and** wife.

16 The words "honor" and "favor" are frequently spelled with a "u" on wedding invitations and announcements. But this is now looked upon as an affectation in this country. and the use of the Americanized form (without the "u") is recommended.

17. The phrase "request the honor of your presence" is always used for church weddings. It may also be used for home, club or hotel weddings—but as such invitations include the reception following the ceremony, the phrase "request the pleasure of your company" is generally considered more suitable.

18. "Wedding breakfast" is the term generally used for the reception following the ceremony if it's before one o'clock in the afternoon. If it's **after** one o'clock "reception" is the correct word to use.

19. At the typical wedding, family and intimate friend are invited to the reception and the ceremony; les intimate friends, neighbors, acquaintances and business associates are invited to the church only. Two sets of invitations may be ordered for the two group of guests: one for the ceremony only, the other fit the ceremony and reception. Or the same invitation may be sent to all guests, with a separate card enclosed for those invited to the reception.
20. When an invitation is for the church ceremony only, a reply is not ordinarily required—and as a rule name is requested. But when the invitation is to both the ceremony and the reception following it, a reply is generally requested. The letters "R.s.v.p." or the phrase "Please reply" may be engraved in the Lower left corner of the invitation; or a separate card to be filled out and returned by the guest may be enclosed.
21. Occasionally, when one of the bride's parents is an invalid, the wedding ceremony is very small and Private, with only the immediate families present; but a big reception follows for all the relatives and friends. In this case, **reception Invitations** only are issued. Invitations to the ceremony are either given verbally to the few who are to be present; or "Ceremony at three o'clock" is written on a small card and enclosed with the invitation to the reception.

ANNOUNCING AN ENGAGEMENT

Engagements are usually announced informally at a luncheon or supper party. Or public announcement is made by writing or telephoning the society editor of the local papers. But occasionally formal announcement of an engagement is sent to members of the family and to friends. The correct wording for an engraved formal announcement follows:

Mr. and Mrs. George Coleman
have the honor to announce
the engagement of their daughter
Harriet
to
Mr. John Anthony Wayne

If the engagement is subsequently broken off, an announcement to that effect must be sent to all who received the original announcement. That's one reason many people prefer to tell the news casually and informally, instead of issuing engraved announcements. But if such announcements **have** been sent out and the engagement is then broken off, an announcement like the following should be sent to the same people:

Mr. and Mrs. George Coleman
wish to announce
that the engagement of their daughter
Harriet
and
Mr. John Anthony Wayne
has been broken by mutual consent

THE CHURCH WEDDING

Here is the correct form for an invitation to a church ceremony:

Mr. and Mrs. Gerald Weylin
request the honor of your presence
at the marriage of their daughter
Margaret
to
Mr. Donald Blaine
on Thursday morning, the seventh of June
at ten o'clock
St. Thomas Episcopal Church
New York

If preferred, the fill-in type of invitation may be used, with space for the guest's name to be written by hand.

Mr. and Mrs. Gerald Weylin
request the honor of
Mr. and Mrs. Alan Brewter's
presence at the marriage of their daughter
Margaret
to
Mr. Donald Blaine
on Thursday, the seventh of June
at ten o'clock in the morning
St. Thomas Episcopal Church
New York

The reception card to go with the above invitation would read as follows:

Mr. and Mrs. Gerald Weylin
request the pleasure of your company
at breakfast
Thursday, the seventh of June
at half past twelve o'clock
Forty-five Park Avenue

Please respond

Or instead of the above form, a small card may be enclosed with the invitation reading simply:

Breakfast
immediately following the ceremony
Forty-five Park Avenue

Please respond

Remember that **"breakfast"** is the proper term for a reception held before one o'clock. . . . **"reception"** is the proper term after one o'clock.

The invitation for an afternoon or evening church

ceremony is exactly the same as the invitation for a morning ceremony—except, of course, for the difference in time. An afternoon invitation would read:

on Thursday, the seventh of June
at four o'clock

or whatever the time may be. An evening invitation would read:

on Thursday evening, the seventh of June
at eight o'clock
or
on Thursday, the seventh of June
at nine o'clock in the evening

There are several types of reception cards suitable for afternoon and evening weddings. The simplest and most familiar type is a card reading:

Reception
at ten o'clock
The St. Moritz

Please send response to
Forty-five Park Avenue

Another popular type of reception card leaves space for the guest's name to be written in:

Mr. and Mrs. Gerald Weylin
request the pleasure of
Mr. and Mrs. Alan Brewster's
company immediately following the ceremony
The St. Moritz

Please address reply to
Forty-five Park Avenue

These cards are enclosed in the envelope with the invitation to the ceremony—for those guests who are invited to both the ceremony and the reception. For guests who are invited to the reception only, an invitation like the following is more acceptable:

Mr. and Mrs. Gerald Weylin
request the pleasure of your company
at the wedding reception of their daughter
Margaret
and
Mr. Donald Blaine
on Thursday, the seventh of June
at four o'clock
The St. Moritz

Please reply to
Forty-five Park Avenue

If all guests, or most of the guests, are invited to both the ceremony at the church and the reception following it, a combined invitation like the following may be used.

Mr. and Mrs. Gerald Weylin
request the honor of your presence
at the marriage of their daughter
Margaret
to
Mr. Donald Blaine
on Thursday, the seventh of June
at twelve o'clock
St. Thomas Episcopal Church
New York
and afterwards at breakfast
at the St. Moritz

Please reply to
Forty-five Park Avenue

Occasionally a reception is given for the bride and groom at the home of a relative or friend. The invitation should be in the name of the bride's parents, regardless of who gives the reception. Here is the correct wording for a card enclosed with the invitation to the ceremony.

Mr. and Mrs. Gerald Weylin
request the pleasure of your company
at the residence of
Mr. and Mrs. John Ridgely
Nine Hundred Riverside Drive
immediately following the ceremony

The reply to such an invitation is always sent to the parents of the bride and not to the people in whose home the reception is held.

CHURCH ADMISSION CARD

When the wedding is large, the church small, and the general public is not to be admitted, cards of admission are necessary for the guests. These are usually engraved in the same style as the invitations, and are enclosed with them. The wording is simply:

Please present this card
at St. Thomas Episcopal Church
on Thursday, the seventh of June

For members of the family and intimate friends, the number of the pew may be written on the admission card in ink. If they are not to occupy individually reserved pews but a special area "ribboned" off at the front ' of the church, the phrase "Within the ribbon" may be written in the lower left corner of the admission card. If admission cards are not necessary, "Pew No. 7" or "Within the ribbon" may be written on a small white card and enclosed with the invitation.

THE HOME WEDDING

The invitation to a **church** wedding is solely for the ceremony, which is why a separate invitation to the wedding breakfast or reception must be enclosed with it. But the invitation to a **home** wedding is for both the ceremony and the reception. Obviously a second invitation to stay on at a house to which the guest is already invited is unnecessary.

Either "honor of your presence" or "pleasure of your company" may be used on the invitation for a home wedding. One is used as much as the other, and both are correct . . . but "honor of your presence" belongs more rightfully to the sacred and solemn dignity of the church.

Here is a typical invitation to a wedding held at the home of the bride:

Mr. and Mrs. Anthony Duncan
request the pleasure of your company
at the marriage of their daughter
Edith Anne
to
Mr. Eugene Griffith
on Tuesday, the tenth of October
at four o'clock
Sixty-four Lake Drive
Chicago, Illinois

The favor of a reply
is requested

If the invitations are issued by the parents of the bride, but the wedding ceremony takes place in a home other than their own, this is the form of invitation to use:

Mr. and Mrs. Anthony Duncan
request the pleasure of your company
at the marriage of their daughter
Edith Anne
to
Mr. Eugene Griffith
on Tuesday, the tenth of October
at four o'clock

at the residence of Mr. and Mrs. John Porter
Twenty-six Ivy Street Chicago, Illinois

If the ceremony is private and guests are invited to the reception only, the following form is used. Note that the word "and" is used instead of "to"—as by the time of the reception the bride and groom are already married.

Mr. and Mrs. Anthony Duncan
request the pleasure of your company
at the wedding reception of their daughter
Edith Anne
and
Mr. Eugene Griffith
on Tuesday, the tenth of October
at eight o'clock
The Drake
Chicago, Illinois

Please send reply to
Sixty-four Lake Drive

For an outdoor wedding, the same form of invitation is used as for any other home wedding . . . except that the phrase "in the garden" appears just above the address. For example:

on Tuesday, the tenth of October
at four o'clock
in the garden
Sixty-four Lake Drive
Chicago, Illinois

As a rule, a rain card is enclosed with the invitation to an outdoor wedding. This is a small card engraved to conform with the invitation, and reads simply:

In the event of rain
the ceremony will be held
at Saint Paul's Church

TRAIN AND DIRECTION CARDS

When a wedding takes place at a country home, the transportation of guests is sometimes arranged by the bride's parents. They may have a special car added to a regular train for the convenience of the guests: or if it's a very big wedding, they may charter a special train for the occasion. Train cards are generally enclosed with the invitation and guests use them in place of tickets. If it's for a special car, this is the best form to use:

A special car will be attached to the train
leaving Pennsylvania Station, New York
for Southampton at 10.40 a.m.
and to the returning training
leaving Southampton at 8.20 p.m.
Please Present this card in place of a ticket

If it's for a special train, this is the way the card is customarily worded:

A special train
on the Long Island Railroad
will leave the Pennsylvania Station, New York
for Southampton at 10.40 a.m.
and returning
will leave Southampton at 8.20 p.m.
Please present this card in place of a ticket

When transportation is not provided, a small card is often enclosed with the invitation to indicate the best trains to take. This is a thoughtful gesture that guests appreciate. The information may be neatly written by hand on plain white cards; or engraved cards for the purpose may be ordered at the same time as the invitations. This is the usual wording:

Train leaves Pennsylvania Station
for Southampton at 10.40 a.m.
Returning train leaves Southampton
for New York at 8.20 p.m.

Route maps and direction cards are also frequently enclosed with the invitation to a country wedding. A simplified map may be printed or engraved on a card for all guests coming from a certain point, like New York. Or a direction card like the following may be used to help guests find their way to the wedding without too much difficulty:

Automobiles from New York follow
Route 27 to Old Town
then turn right at the white arrow
and follow Hedgerow Road
to Shady Acres

Train and direction cards do not need to be enclosed in separate envelopes. They are merely slipped into the same envelope as the invitation. However, it's a good idea to use sheets of tissue between the cards and the invitation to prevent smudging. Suitable tissue for this purpose very thin and in the proper size—can be provided by your stationer.

WEDDING ANNOUNCEMENTS

When a wedding is small and private and no general invitations are issued, it is customary to send out formal announcements on the day of the ceremony or very soon afterward. Such announcements should have all the traditional beauty and dignity of wedding invitations-being engraved on the finest white paper and, like invitations, enclosed in two envelopes.

The announcement is made by whoever would have sent out the wedding invitations. That means the parents or nearest relative, whether actually present at the ceremony or not. For example, even if the bride's mother is an invalid even if her father is abroad at the time of the ceremony-the announcements are issued in the names of both parents.

Announcements are never sent to those who were present at the ceremony. Nor are they sent **instead** of invitations to relatives and friends living at a great distance. An **invitation** sent to someone far away means, "We would have loved to have you with us!" But an **announcement** means, "We couldn't invite you to the wedding, but we want you to know about it."

Here is the correct wording for a formal wedding announcement:

Mr. and Mrs. Anthony Duncan
have the honor of announcing
the marriage of their daughter
Edith Anne
to
Mr. Eugene Griffith
on Tuesday, the tenth of October
Nineteen hundred and sixty
Saint Paul's Church
Chicago, Illinois

Instead of "honor of announcing" it is also correct to use "honor to announce" or just "announce." For example, here is the form customarily used for announcements after an elopement. Notice that the name of the city or town in which the ceremony was held is given; but the name of the church or the house address where the ceremony was performed is not necessary (though it is frequently included):

Mr. and Mrs. Clyde Peters
announce the marriage of their daughter
Marion
to
Mr. Nelson Crowinshield
on Friday, the twentieth of June
Nineteen hundred and sixty
Carson City, Nevada

If the bride is a young widow or divorcee, the announcement is still made in the name of her parents or nearest kin:

Mr. and Mrs. Clyde Peters
announce the marriage of their daughter
Marion Peters Armstrong

to

Mr. Nelson Crowinshield
on Friday, the twentieth of June
Nineteen hundred and sixty
Carson City, Nevada

But if the widow or divorcee is a woman of mature years the announcement may be made in her own name and that of the groom, as follows:

Mrs. Helen Wallace Smith

and

Mr. William Tracy Hamilton
announce their marriage
on Friday, the twenty-first of May
Nineteen hundred and sixty
at Saratoga Springs, New York

Ordinarily "Mrs." isn't used before the name of a widow or divorcee on an announcement of her remarriage, when the announcement is Issued by her parents or other relatives. But it is **always** used on announcements issued by the bride and groom themselves.

ENCLOSING "AT HOME" CARDS WITH THE ANNOUNCEMENT

If the bride and groom want to let their friends know where they are going to live, they send them cards of address—or as they are more familiarly called. "at home' cards. These are usually enclosed with the announcements of the marriage; or they are sent out separately after the bride and groom are settled in their own home and ready to receive visitors.

The typical at home card is about the size of a visiting card and reads:

> Mr. and Mrs. Eugene Griffith
> will be at home
> after the first of November
> at Twenty-five Little Plains Road

Or a joint visiting card of the new "Mr. and Mrs." may be used, with the address indicated in the lower right corner:

> Mr. and Mrs. Eugene Griffith
>
> 25 Little Plains Road

At home cards engraved with the bride's new name should not be sent out **before** the ceremony-for the reason, of course, that she has not yet acquired her new name. However, cards without any name may be enclosed with the invitations. These would read:

> At home
> after the first of November
> Twenty-five Little Plains Road

WEDDING INVITATIONS FOR SPECIAL AND UNUSUAL CIRCUMSTANCES

Not all weddings conform to type, and those involving Trial or unusual circumstances-such as the bride with one parent, the bride whose parents have remarried, the double wedding for sisters, and so on—require special wedding of the invitation.

The forms that follow are for these special cases' and though they are for invitations, they apply also to wedding **announments** issued under the same circumstances.

INVITATION TO A DOUBLE WEDDING

Mr. and Mrs. Henry Hassett
request the honor of your presence
at the marriage of their daughters
Nancy Joan
to
Mr. Robert Kinnaird

and

Amy Jean
to
Mr. Harrison Colt
on Friday, the second of October
at four o'clock
Grace Church
Brookline, Massachusetts

Sometimes friends or cousins are married on the same, day, at the same time, and invitations are issued jointly for both ceremonies. The wording of a double wedding invitation when the brides are **not** sisters should include confusion:

Mr. and Mrs. Henry Hassett
and
Mr. and Mrs. John Ward Sheldon

request the honor of your presence
at the marriage of their daughters
Nancy Joan Hassett
to
Mr. Robert Kinnaird

and
Marion Sheldon
to
Mr. Frederick Bowen
on Thursday, the fourth of October
at four o'clock
Grace Church
Brookline, Massachusetts

THE BRIDE WITH ONE PARENT

If a bride's mother is dead and her father has not remarried the invitations are issued in his name alone:

Mr. James Norman Walsh
requests the honor of your presence
at the marriage of his daughter
Edith

to

Mr. Curtis Phelps
and so forth

If the bride's father is dead and her mother has not remarried the invitations are issued in the name of the mother.

But if the mother **has** remarried and the bride has a stepfather, the invitations are issued in the names of both. Following are the two forms that are most frequently used. Both are correct; the choice is entirely a matter of personal preference. The bride's **full name** should always be used; and in the first of the two forms given below, "her daughter" may be used instead of "their daughter."

Mr. and Mrs. Benjamin Crane
request the honor of your presence
at the marriage of their daughter
Mary Alice Thorne
and so forth

or

Mr. and Mrs. Benjamin Crane
request the honor of your presence
at the marriage of
Mrs. Crane's daughter
Mary Alice Thorne
and so forth

If the bride has a stepmother, the invitations may read "the marriage of their daughter," "the marriage of his daughter," or "the marriage of Mr. Walsh's daughter" depending on which wording best suits the circumstances and the wishes of those most intimately concerned. In this instance, of course, the bride's full name does not need to be used as it's the same as the name in which the invitations are issued.

WHEN THE PARENTS OF THE BRIDE ARE DIVORCED

Parents who are divorced and remarried do **not**, under any circumstances, combine their different names on invitations or announcements for their daughter's marriage. It's not only a question of taste and propriety. The names of divorced parents and their new mates appearing together on a wedding invitation is an affront to the sacred dignity of marriage.

Invitations should be issued in the name of,the parent with whom the bride has been living. If that parent has remarried, the invitations are issued in the names of the parent **and** the new mate. If the bride has lived part of the time with one parent and part of the time with the other, the invitations are usually issued in the name of the mother.

Here is the wording to use when the bride's mother is a divorcee who has not remarried:

Mrs. Preston Hodges
requests the honor of your presence
at the marriage of her daughter
Carolyn
and so forth

Here is the wording to use when the bride's mother is a divorcee who **has** remarried:

Mr. and Mrs. Ronald Fischer
request the honor of your presence
at the marriage of her daughter
Carolyn Hodges
and so forth

or

Mr. and Mrs. Ronald Fischer
request the honor of your presence
at the marriage of
Mrs. Fischer's daughter
Carolyn Hodges
and so forth

WHEN THE BRIDE HAS NO PARENTS

As a rule, when a bride has no parents the invitations are issued by her oldest brother, whether he is married or not. Or a sister, aunt, grandparent or other close relative gives the wedding and issues the invitations. If there are no relatives and no guardian, the invitations may be issued by intimate friends. And in those rare cases when there are neither relatives nor friends to issue the invitations, the bride and groom invite their own guests—using the form immediately below:

The honor of your presence
is requested at the marriage of
Miss Laura Ellen Kay
to
Mr. Thomas Field Macfarlane
on Thursday the eighteenth of June
at twelve o'clock
Trinity Church
Detroit, Michigan

When wedding invitations are issued by a married brother and sister-in-law of the bride, this is the proper wording:

Mr. and Mrs. Henry Fairchild
request the honor of your presence
at the marriage of their sister
Janet Fairchild
to
Mr. William Pierce
on Friday, the third of October
at four o'clock
Grace Church
Brookline, Massachusetts

Following is the correct forth to use when a married sister and brother-in-law give the wedding and issue the invitations:

Mr. and Mrs. John Alan Wright
request the honor of your presence
at the marriage of their sister
Eleanor Rogers
to
Mr. Frank Pearson
on Wednesday, the first of June
at four o'clock

Saint Paul's Church
Seattle, Washington

When friends give a wedding reception at their home for a bride who has no parents, this is the way the invitation should read:

Mr. and Mrs. Maxwell Burton
request the pleasure of your company
at the wedding reception of
Miss Martha Heistrom
and
Mr. Raymond Frank Peterson
at four o'clock
Six Beach Lane Road
Manhasset, Long Island

Please respond

INVITATIONS FOR A SECOND MARRIAGE

If a widow or divorcee is young, the invitations to her second marriage are issued in the name of her parents or nearest relative; and the form is the same as for her first wedding except that the full name is used. For example:

Mr. and Mrs. Henry Hassett
request the honor of your presence
at the marriage of their daughter
Nancy Hassett Kinnaird
to
Mr. William Kingston
and so forth

If the bride is a mature woman, or if there are no relatives or old family friends to issue the invitations, this form is acceptable:

The honor of your presence is requested
at the marriage of
Mrs. Nancy Hassett Kinnaird
and
Mr. William Kingston
and so forth

The name of the bride always comes first on invitations and announcements issued by the bride and groom.

A divorcee uses whatever name she has taken after the divorce. If she has legally resumed her maiden name, it is entirely permissible for her to use it on the invitations and announcements of her second marriage.

WHEN THE GROOM IS IN THE MILITARY SERVICES

The generally accepted rule at present is that for the rank of Captain or above in the Army-Lieutenant, senior grade, or above in the Navy-the title is used in front of the name. For example:

Captain Arthur Cunningham,
United States Army

For officers under these ranks, the title goes on a line directly below the name. For example:

Harold Creighton
Lieutenant, junior grade, United States Navy

If the groom is in the regular Army or Navy, the wording "United States Army" (or Navy) appears in the line below his name. But if he has been called into the Army or given a temporary commission, the positioning is the same but the wording is "Army of the United States"-or for the Navy, "United States Naval Reserve." In the case of a private or non-commissioned officer, the name is on one line and the branch of service is designated below it. For example:

Frank Pearson
Signal Corps, United States Naval Reserve
or
John Hamilton
Coast Artillery, Army of the United States

The title of "Mr." is not used in military invitations or announcements.

Army Officer's Wedding Invitation

Colonel and Mrs. Charles Higgins
request the honor of your presence
at the marriage of their daughter
Marilyn
to
Captain Richard Anderson
United States Army
on Tuesday, the tenth of October
at four o'clock
Christ Church
Santa Barbara, California

Army Officer's Wedding Announcement

Mr. and Mrs. John Curtis
announce the marriage of their daughter
Catherine Alice
to
David Alan Sewall
Second Lieutenant, United States Army
on Thursday, the seventh of September
Nineteen hundred and sixty
Boston, Massachusetts

Naval Officer's Wedding Invitation

Mr. and Mrs. Winston Evans
request the honor of your presence
at the marriage of their daughter
Marion Elaine
to
Theodore Spencer
Ensign, United States Navy
on Friday, the first of August
at twelve o'clock
Saint Paul's Church
New York

Naval Officer's Wedding Announcemmt

Mr. and Mrs. Thomas Rourke
announce the marriage of their daughter
Adelaide
to
Commander Ralph Cummings
United States Navy
on Thursday, the seventh of June
Nineteen hundred and sixty
Trinity Church
Washington, District of Columbia

RECALLING A WEDDING INVITATION

A sudden death in the family, serious illness or an accident may make it necessary to recall the invitations issued for a wedding. If it's very close to the date set for the wedding, someone in the family should notify immediately all who received invitations. But if there's time. small cards should be printed or engraved and sent to the list of expected guests. The announcement should be formal in wording, but is not necessarily arranged with indented lines.

The reason for recalling the invitation is always given:

> Owing to the sudden death of
> Mr. Donald Blaine's sister,
> Mr. and Mrs. Gerald Weylin beg
> to recall the invitations issued
> for the marriage of their
> daughter, Margaret, on Thursday
> the seventh of June.

or

> Mr. and Mrs. Gerald Weylin
> regret that owing to their daughter's
> illness they are obliged to recall
> the invitations to her marriage
> on Thursday, the seventh of June.

When a wedding is broken off after the invitations have been issued, announcements should be sent out as quickly as possible. If comparatively few guests are expected—or if time is short—someone close to the bride (preferably her mother) should telephone the people who must be notified. No explanation need be given on the telephone or in the announcement; just a matter-of-fact statement that the wedding will not take place is all that's necessary:

> Mr. and Mrs. Gerald Weylin announce
> that the marriage of their daughter
> Margaret and Mr. Donald Blaine
> will not take place.

HOW TO ACKNOWLEDGE WEDDING INVITATIONS

An invitation to a church wedding does not require written acknowledgment-unless a reply is specifically requested, or unless an invitation to the reception is included. But a prompt acceptance or regret **is** definitely required for a home, club or hotel wedding, or for an invitation to a wedding reception.

The answer to a formal wedding invitation should not be written like a friendly note, but should be in formal third-person phraseology. It may be written in straight box form, without indented margins, if that is preferred; but the wording should follow the exact wording of the invitation even to the repetition of date, place and time. That helps prevent the possibility of a misunderstanding. A **regret**, of course, does not require repetition of the time, as that is unimportant if one does not plan to attend.

It's thoughtless and rude to wait until two or three days before the wedding to mail your acceptance or regret. Always write your reply and mail it **promptly**, within a few clays after receiving the invitation. Write it by hand, on the first page of a double sheet of your best white note paper.

Here is the correct form to use for accepting a formal invitation to a reception following the ceremony:

Mr. and Mrs. Edward Willis
accept with pleasure
Mr. and Mrs. Anton Duncan's
kind invitation for
Tuesday, the tenth of October
at eight o'clock
at the Drake

Or it may be written without the indented arrangement of the lines:

Mr. and Mrs. Edward Willis accept
with pleasure Mr. and Mrs. Anthony
Duncan's kind, invitation for Tuesday,
the tenth of October at
eight o'clock, at the Drake.

Whenever possible, the regret should include a reason for not being able to accept:

Mr. and Mrs. Edward Willis
regret that a previous engagement
prevents their accepting
Mr. and Mrs. Anthony Duncan's
kind invitation for
Tuesday, the tenth of October

A combined invitation to the ceremony and reception would be acknowledged as follows:

Mr. and Mrs. Edward Willis
accept with pleasure
Mr. and Mrs. Anthony Duncan's
kind invitation to be present
at the marriage of their daughter
Edith Anne
to
Mr. Eugene Griffith
on Tuesday, the tenth of October
at four o'clock
and afterward at the wedding reception
at the Drake

Regret

Mr. and Mrs. Edward Willis
regret exceedingly that
owing to the illness of their son
they are unable to accept
Mr. and Mrs. Anthony Duncan's
kind invitation to be present
at the marriage of their daughter
Edith Anne
to
Mr. Eugene Griffith
on Tuesday, the tenth of October
and afterward at the wedding reception

The **announcement** of a wedding does not call for farewell acknowledgment, like an invitation. You may write a note of congratulation, if you like (see page 173). or you may send a wedding gift if that is your generous irnpulse. But these are entirely of your own pleasure and volition; no response is required.

THE INFORMAL WEDDING INVITATION WRITTEN BY HAND

Personal notes are written when the wedding is very small and informal, and only a few relatives and intimate friends are invited. They should be written **by hand**, on plain white paper—preferably double sheets like those used for engraved invitations. Colored, decorated or odd shaped stationery, or correspondence cards, are not good taste even for the most informal wedding invitations.

These little notes of invitation to a small and intimate wedding should always be written by the bride herself. Even if she is extremely busy (as most brides are before their wedding!) she should not ask a sister or a friend to write the notes for her. No one is ever too busy to write a few short notes to those they care enough about to want at a small, intimate, wedding ceremony.

There is one exception to the rule that the bride always writes her own notes of invitation. If the bride's mother has an old and cherished friend, she may want to write her about the plans and invite her personally to **her** daughter's wedding. Here is an example:

Dear Martha:

At last my Helen has set the day! She and David are to be married very quietly at the Community Church on Thursday, June the twelfth, at noon. They have invited just a very few relatives and intimate friends, and they are all coming here after the ceremony for a simple little wedding breakfast I'm planing for them.

Helen had your name at the very top of her guest list, but I said I'd write to you myself. We'll see you at the church at twelve, Martha-and of course we expect you to come back here with us afterward for the wedding breakfast.

I am very happy, as you can imagine. I am already as devoted to David as though he were my own son!

Affectionately yours,
Sarah

Bride's Note of Invitation to a Close Friend

Dear Betty:

David and I have set the date—and we want you to be the first to know it! We're going to be married **very quietly** at the Community Church on Thursday, June the twelfth, at noon. We're asking only a few people—just our nearest relatives and our very special friends.

Can you be at the house about eleven, Betty, and go to the church with us? Then we'll all come back here after the ceremony; mother's giving a little wedding breakfast for us.

Let's hope it's a bright sunny day on the twelfth! With much love,

Helen

To a relative

Dear Aunt Kate:

David and I are to be married at the Community Church on Thursday, June the twelfth, at noon.

We want you to come to the ceremony, and also to the wedding breakfast afterward at home.

We'll be looking for you, Aunt Kate, on the twelfth!

With love,
Helen

If There Has Been a Recent Bereavement

Dear Julia:

We have changed our plans for an elaborate church wedding because of the death of my uncle.

Instead, Bill and I are going to be married very simply and quietly at my home on Sunday. June the sixth, at four o'clock. We have invited only those we love best, and of course we want you!

There will be a small supper party at six, so plan to stay on for the evening.

Affectionately,
Grace

To an Old friend of the Groom —a Stranger to the Bride

Dear Mr. Knox:

Paul Lawrence and I are to be married on Sunday. May the eighth, at the Presbyterian Church on Main Street in Lenox. The ceremony will be at three o'clock.

I know Lenox is a long way from Philadelphia, but we would both love to have you come if you can possibly make it. Paul has spoken so often and so fondly of his old roommate at Exerter that I feel as through I know you! I am looking forward with very great pleasure to meeting you at last.

So **do** come if you can, and stay on for the small reception at my home in the evening. There is a train that leaves here at 9:20 and would get you back to Philadelphia before midnight.

It will make us both very happy to have you come to our wedding!

Sincerely yours,
Marjorie Willis

TO A BUSINESS ASSOCIATE OF THE GROOM

The bride writes all the notes of invitation, including those to business associates of the groom. If a business associate is married, the note should be addressed to his wife. For example:

Dear Mrs. Harris:

Frank Peters and I are to be married at my home on Tuesday, October the fourth, at eight o'clock in the evening.

Frank has been so long and so happily associated with Mr. Harris, that the wedding just wouldn't be complete without him! We hope you can both come, and that you will stay on for the small reception following the ceremony.

Sincerely yours,
Catherine Miller

INVITING A FRIEND TO THE RECEPTION ONLY

Dear Harriet:

Jim and I are going to be married on Friday morning, June the twentieth.

In view of circumstances with which you are familiar, the ceremony will be **very private** ... with only my sister and one of Bill's friends as witnesses.

But we are having a small reception at the Terrace Club on the evening of the twentieth, at eight o'clock, and we want you to come. We are asking only a few of our best friends. Bill wants me to say he's as anxious to have you come as I am.

So we'll see you, won't we, Harriet—Friday at eight at the Terrace Club!

Affectionately yours,
Madeline

Informal notes of invitation like the above should be answered promptly, briefly and with a definite acceptance or regret. Sometimes relatives or friends telephone to say whether or not they are coming ... and while that's not incorrect, it may be **inconvenient** for a busy bride and her mother to receive many calls. It is always more gracious to answer a note of invitation with a note.

TYPICAL NOTE OF ACCEPTANCE

Dear Grace:

Of course I'll come to your wedding on Sunday, June the sixth, at four o'clock—and stay on for the party in the evening. I wouldn't miss it for anything!

Thanks, darling, for including me among the friends you like best! My love to you and Jim; and I hope the sixth is a bright, beautiful day for your wedding.

Affectionately,
Julia

TYPICAL NOTE OF REGRET

Dear Miss Miller:

Mr. Harris and I regret exceedingly that we cannot accept your kind invitation for Tuesday, October the fourth.

It was sweet of you to ask us to your wedding, and we'd love to come; but unfortunately we will be in Baltimore on the fourth for our grandson's christening, and we won't be able to get back in time for your wedding.

We hope to meet Frank Peters' bride very soon; and in the meantime, we send you both our best wishes for a lifetime of happiness together!

Sincerely yours.
Dorothea Harris

INVITATIONS TO WEDDING ANNIVERSARIES

If the celebration of a wedding anniversary is simple and informal, the invitations are written by hand or are telephoned. Here is the way a note of invitation to a twenty-fifth anniversary buffet supper might be written:

Dear Alice:

Tom and I will be married twenty-five years next Thursday, June the tenth—and we want our friends to help us celebrate.

We're having a buffet supper with dancing afterward—and we hope you and John can come. Supper will be at eight.

We'll be looking for you on the tenth, Alice!

Affectionately yours,
Betty

Acceptance

Dear Betty:

It's hard to believe you and Tom have been married twenty-five years! I wish I knew your secret of staying so **young-looking!**

John and I will be delighted to come and help you celebrate your anniversary. We'll be there Thursday. June the tenth, at eight.

In the meantime, our love and congratulations to you both—and our best wishes for the long years of happiness still ahead!

Affectionately yours
Alice

Regret

Dear Betty:

I wish we could come to your party on Thursday, the

tenth, but we have already accepted a dinner engagement for that evening and I don't think we could get out of it without considerable embarrassment.

John and I would have loved to come and help you celebrate your anniversary, but we'll be with you in spirit, Betty! And we send you and Tom our congratulations and very best wishes for continued happiness in the years ahead!

Affectionately,
Alice

Frequently a formal reception is given to celebrate a twenty-fifth-or fiftieth wedding anniversary. The invitations are engraved, and usually the year of the wedding and the year of the anniversary are given at the top. These significant dates—or even the entire invitation, if so desired—may be engraved in silver lettering for a twenty-fifth anniversary, in gold lettering, for a fiftieth anniversary. Following are the two forms generally used for an afternoon reception. The wording is the same for an evening reception, except for the time, and if it's a dinner or a supper dance, that fact is of course specified.

19 19

Mr. and Mrs. Edward Paul Sullivan
request the pleasure of your company
on the Fiftieth Anniversary of their marriage
on Thursday, the seventh of October
from four until seven o'clock
The Inn
Andover, Massachusetts

19 -19

Mr. and Mrs. Edward Paul Sullivan
At Home

on Thursday, the seventh of October
from four until seven o'clock

The Inn
Andover, Massachusetts

These invitations are answered like all other formal invitations: a definite acceptance or regret in the same precise, third-person phraseology—handwritten on plain white note paper of good quality:

Mr. and Mrs. John Wolfe
accept with pleasure
Mr. and Mrs. Edward Paul Sullivan's
kind invitation
for Thursday, the seventh of October
from four until seven o'clock
at the Inn
Andover.

❒ ❒ ❒ ❒ ❒

Chapter VII

LETTERS OF THANKS

ONE kind of letter most people enjoy writing is the letter of thanks or appreciation. It's pleasant to say "thank you" to someone who has been generous or thoughtful.

Every gift, however trifling, should be acknowledged with a note of thanks. Every favor or courtesy-every kindness or attention on the part of a neighbour or friend every expression of hospitality—certainly every letter of condolence or congratulation reserves sincere and gracious acknowledgment.

And it doesn't matter if you have already expressed your appreciation in person; a letter of thanks must still be written! It can be as brief and simple as you like; but it should express your appreciation with sincerity and warmth. Remember that half the joy of giving is the anticipation of receiving pleased acknowledgment; and surely the person who has been thoughtful or generous toward you deserves that satisfaction! Forgotten thank you notes can soon make **you** forgotten when you'd like very much to be remembered.

Sincerity is by far the most important quality of all in a note of thanks. If it's just a run-of-the-mill "duty" note-a brief but uninspired thank-you written because such a note is expected and must be written-it defeats its own purpose. It does not give the pleasure and satisfaction a note of thanks should give.

So be sure your letter has the unmistakable ring, of sincerity to it. That's much easier to accomplish when you feel grateful and appreciative than it is later on when the emotion has cooled and the enthusiasm worn off. The whole secret is this: **don't wait too long to write your note of**

thanks! Don't procrastinate and keep putting it off. Write your letter quickly . . . while the glow is still with you! Then you won't need to grope for words, trying to sound sincere. The words will come of their own accord, will spring naturally and sincerely from the warmth of your own enthusiasm.

We cannot tell you the exact words to put in your personal letters of thanks. After all, the very essence of sincerity is the expression of your own true feelings and sentiments. But we **can** make suggestions. And that, precisely, is what you will find in this chapter: suggestions we hope will prove helpful and stimulating when you "just don't know what to write!"

WHEN AND HOW TO ACKNOWLEDGE WEDDING GIFTS

As soon as the wedding invitations go out, the gifts start coming in. And the smart bride starts writing her notes of thanks right away, as each gift arrives. She doesn't wait until the thank-you's pile up and get ahead of her, becoming a problem instead of a pleasure.

The bride who is systematic as well as smart, keeps a little gift book. It may be one of the handsome, little books that are published for this purpose and kept as a souvenir ... or it may be just a blank notebook like children use at school. In it she records each gift as it arrives: what it is, from whom it came, the sender's address, where the gift was purchased, when the note of thanks was written and mailed. Then she never needs to wonder, "Did I ever thank Aunt Mary for the picture?" Or, "Did I over write and acknowledge Uncle Pete's check?"

Then, too, if the bride is swamped with gifts a few days before the wedding, and it just isn't humanly possible to write all the necessary thank-you's in time, she can take the gift book along on the honeymoon and write the notes while she's away. Of course, If she's only going to be gone a week or two, the notes can wait. But if she's going to be away for a month or more, she should take the list with her and write the notes of thanks as soon as she can. This is a task that cannot be evaded . . . nor should any gracious bride want to evade writing cordial notes to those who showered her so generously with gifts!

The bride acknowledges all gifts, for her husband and herself-including gifts from friends or business associates of her husband whom she has never seen and doesn't know. All notes must be personally written by the bride herself; she cannot relegate someone else to do it for her. If gifts arrive while she is away, her mother may acknowledge them-but only to say: "Helen had already gone when your beautiful gift arrived. She will, of course, write and thank you as soon as she gets back." Or better still. the mother may write to the bride and describe the gift so that she can acknowledge it herself. This isn't necessary, of course, if the bride will be back in a reasonable time.

Printed or engraved cards of thanks won't do for wedding gifts-or any gifts! They are not sincere, and they are not in good taste. A letter and **only a letter** in the bride's own handwriting is correct for thanking relatives and friends for their wedding gifts. These thank-you's should be written on formal paper-not on cards or so called "informals." There is no objection to the use of "informals!' for brief notes to friends, acknowledgments of kindness or hospitality, even for invitations to card parties and other simple home functions; but they should not be used for acknowledging wedding gifts.

The bride's, notes should be an expression of her own personality; but the following provide a variety of acceptable Patterns from which she can easily design her own.

To Relatives

Dear Aunt Kate:

It's hard to believe I've been married two whole weeks,

and here we are—David and I—in our own lovely home!

One of the things we enjoy most, Aunt Kate, is using the simply **luscious** bath linens you gave us! It was a generous gift, and David and I send you our love and our thanks.

You must come real soon and see how beautifully your Linens go with the colors in our bathroom!

With love,
Helen

Dear Aunt Mary and Uncle Jim:

When I unpacked your gift today. I was so thrilled I was practically **speechless!** How did you two darlings know I love Spode and would rather have it than any other kind of china? It's such a very lovely pattern; I can hardly wait to show it off to my friends!

David is as delighted as I am. We have decided that you shall be our very first dinner guests so that you can see for yourselves how beautiful our table looks all dressed up in your Spode!

Thank you for your generous gift and for the sweet note that came with it. David and I send you our love!

Affectionately yours,
Helen

When a present is sent by a married couple, the note of thanks may be written to both-as above-or it may be written to the wife alone, with thanks to both in the letter. For example, here is a typical note of thanks to a married cousin:

Dear Margaret:

Thank you so much for the perfectly **beautiful** little boudoir clock you and Bill sent us! it's one of the very nicest wedding gifts we have received.

David sends thanks too; we hope you'll come soon and see how lovely the clock looks on our dresser. You just couldn't have made a better choice!

With love from both of us,

Helen

Bachelor uncles are usually very generous. This letter is to a favorite uncle who sent an expensive silver tea service:

Uncle Joe, darling!

I'll be the proudest hostess in all New York when I use my handsome tea service! What a simply **magnificent** gift-and how, generous of you to select it for David and me! We were quite overwhelmed when we unpacked it this morning. It's standing on the table right near me as I write this note, and I keep looking at it and **gloating** because it's really and truly mine!

Thank you, darling-for David and me. We're expecting you to be a **very frequent visitor** at our house, and don't think for a minute well let you disappoint us!

Love from both of us, and a special hug and kiss from me.

Helen

To Intimate Friends

Joan, dear:

Thank you so much for the beautiful candy jar It looks so attractive on our cotter table-you must come and see for yourself.

David and I deeply appreciate your gift, Joan, and we send you our thanks and our affection!

Devotedly,
Helen

Dearest Carolyn:

I just can't get over the English hunting prints you sent us! They're exactly what David and I want for our dining room; but we didn't think we'd be lucky enough to get them as a gift!

David and I are delighted, Carolyn. Thank you very, very much!

We're looking, forward to seeing you at the wedding.

Affectionately yours,
Helen

It's always more gracious to mention the specific gift. example, don't write, "Thanks for the beautiful gift" but "Thanks for the beautiful lamp." And it's nice to mention something special about the gift if possible-how it just goes with something else, or just fits into a certain decorative scheme, or is in some other way the perfect choice. People like to be told they selected the ideal gift: it's part of the pleasure of giving we mentioned earlier in the chapter.

Dear Betty:

You couldn't have selected a more **perfect** gift for David and me if you had tried! We've been looking for twin lamps for our twin night tables; but we haven't seen anything to compare with the ones you sent. They are gorgeous, Betty—and the turquoise shades will go beautifully with the draperies and spreads we ordered.

It was Generous of you to sees such a wonderful gift. I just don't know how to thank you! David says to be sure and tell you how delighted **he** is with the lamps, too.

Affectionately yours,
Helen

A gift received from an intimate friend of the groom should be acknowledged by the bride, of course. And although she does not know him well, her letter should be very friendly and cordial . . . as she is writing for the groom and herself. A well-written note of thanks is enthusiastic but not profuse.

Dear Bob:

How very sweet of you to send David and me such a beautiful pair of candlesticks! We're delighted with them, and we just can't thank you enough.

David and I are looking forward to seeing you Tuesday at the wedding.

Thanks again for your **wonderful** gift!

Affectionately,
Helen

To Less Intimate Friends

Dear Margaret:

David and I are delighted with the beautiful vase you sent us. We plan to give it a place of honor in our living room.

It was sweet of you to send such a lovely gift, and we both thank you very much.

Sincerely,
Helen Curtis

Dear Miss Walsh:

Thank you for the lovely, lovely salad bowl! I'm sure it will be one of our most useful gifts. David said to be sure and send **his** thanks, too!

With best wishes from both of us.

Cordially yours,
Helen Curtis

Dear Mrs. Chalmers:

We just **love** the tray you sent us! David says it's one of the most beautiful trays he has ever seen . . and I certainly agree with him.

Thank you very much!

Sincerely,
Helen Curtis

Neighbors who were not invited to the wedding but who sent a gift should receive an especially cordial note of thanks:

Dear Mrs. Howland:

It was most kind of you and Mr. Howland to send us a gift—and such a handsome one! We are simply **thrilled** with the book ends; they are just what we needed for our library desk.

We hope that you and Mr. Howland will come real soon, and see for yourselves how beautiful the book ends look.

Cordially yours,
Helen Curtis

To a Friend in Mourning

Dearest Emily:

David and I were deeply touched when your gift arrived today. With all you have on your heart and mind right now, it was sweet of you to thank of us. . . .

Thank you, darling. The luncheon cloth is lovely, and we appreciate it more than we can say!

Devotedly,
Helen

To a Friend Far Away

Dear Claire:

What a wonderful surprise to receive your gift today—all the way from Italy! And what a perfectly **beautiful** pair of figurines! I love them, Claire—and I just don't know how to thank you for them.

David joins me in sending thanks for your lovely gift, and

for your thoughtfulness in remembering us when you are so far away. We're sorry you won't be here for the wedding, but we'll be thinking of you!

With love from us both,

Affectionately.
Helen

To a Business Associate of the Groom

Dear Mr. Kingston:

Thank you for the beautiful carving set you sent David and me. It's a lovely gift, and a useful one-and we appreciate it very much.

Sincerely yours,
Helen Curtis

If the card accompanying the gift is from "Mr. and Mrs. Kingston," the note of thanks should be addressed to Mrs. Kingston—even though neither the bride nor groom know her personally. If Mr. Kingston does not customarily address the groom by his first name, it's advisable to use his surname in the note of thanks. The use of first name or surname in any note of thanks depends upon the degree of intimacy between the persons involved.

Dear Mrs. Kingston:

I want to thank you and Mr. Kingston for the beautiful carving set you sent Mr. Johnson and me. It's a lovely gift, and a useful one-and we appreciate it very much indeed!

Sincerely yours,
Helen Curtis

To an Old Classmate of the Groom —a Stranger to the Bride

Dear Mr. Foster:

David and I think it was most generous of you to send

us such a beautiful gift! We love the little carved Chinese figures, and they'll be just **perfect** on our mantel!

I'm delightod to know you are coming to New York for the wedding. David has talked of you so often, and with such great affection, that I'm looking forward to meeting you.

Many thanks for the gift, from David and me!

Sincerely yours,
Helen Curtis

SHOWER GIFTS SHOULD BE INDIVIDUALLY ACKNOWLEDGED

When an engaged girl is given a shower of gifts by her friends, it's not enough to express verbal thank at the party. An individual note of thanks should be written to each person who contributed a gift.

Dear Anne:

I was so thrilled and excited on Saturday that I'm sure I didn't thank you adequately for the beautiful guest towels. They are lovely—and exactly the color I would have selected myself!

Thanks so much, Anne. I'm looking forward to seeing you on the twelfth.

Affectionately,
Janet

A special note of thanks goes to the hostess who planned the party and provided the refreshments:

Susan, dear:

You were sweet to give a shower for me, and I appreciate it more than I can say. I don't know how you managed to keep it such a secret! It was a complete surprise to me . . . and a thrill I'll never forget.

Bill and I are overwhelmed by the wealth of lovely lines

we have suddenly received. Your tea cloth is especially lovely, Susan. I am **doubly** indebted to you -for tho party and for your generous gift!

Thanks form both of us — to a swell gal and a wonderful friend!

With love,
Janet

NOTES OF THANKS FOR CHRISTMAS GIFTS

Instead of a run-of-the-mill note that merely acknowledges the gift you received and says a casual "thank you"—try to show real appreciation. You can do that by pointing out certain features of the gift that especially appeal to you. Or you can tactfully point out that it's just what you've been wanting—just what you've been hoping for. The point is to make the person who sent the gift feel that it is a very good selection, that you are delighted and pleased with it.

Dear Aunt Mary:

What a simply **gorgeous** Christmas gift! A fitted bag is something I've wanted **for a** long time, but could never get for myself.

Thank you so much, Aunt Mary. I'll have the bag for years and years, and I'll think of you with gratitude and affection every time I use it.

Lovingly yours,
Carolyn

Dear Irene:

I'm delighted with the bracelet you sent me for Christmas. Imagine! It just matches a pair of earrings my sister gave me. Isn't that a lucky coincidence?

You certainly made an inspired choice, Irene! **I love** the bracelet and can't think of anything I'd rather have had. Thank you very much.

Affectionately,
Carolyn

Dear Bob:

How did you know my favorite brand of candy? It's the one kind I just never can resist!

It was thoughtful of you to remember me at Christmas, Bob, and I appreciate it very much.

Cordially yours,
Carolyn

Dear Mrs. Carter:

John and I have been displaying your Christmas gift with great pleasure and pride.

The cups and saucers are **exquisite**—and we think it was wonderful of you to remember that collecting Spode is our hobby.

Many thanks to you and Mr. Carter for your thoughtful and generous gift, and our best wishes to you for the new year!

Sincerely yours,
Carolyn Brewster

FOR BIRTHDAY GIFT

Dear Alice:

If you had asked me what 1 wanted for my birthday, I'd have said, "A charm for my bracelet." You just couldn't have selected anything I'd like more!

The little stagecoach is adorable—I can't wait to have it put on the bracelet. Isn't it cute the way the tiny wheels turn?

Thank you, Alice. You have a positive **genius** for selecting the right gift!

With love,
Dorothy

Dear Jean:

You never forget my birthday, do you? No wonder you are my favorite cousin!

The scarf is lovely, and it's just what I needed to go with my new suit. The colors are so soft and flattering!

Thank you, darling-not only for the scarf, but for the very sweet card that came with it.

Lovingly yours,
Dorothy

Dear Arthur:

I'm writing this note on the lovely stationery you sent me for my birthday. It was sweet of you to remember, and I want you to know that I appreciate it.

Many thanks, Arthur—for the gift and for your good wishes!

Sincerely,
Dorothy

Dear Uncle Pete:

I thought I told you I was going to stop having birthdays...After all, a girl doesn't like being reminded she's a year older!

But how can I scold you when you've been so generous? The pen is a beauty, Uncle Pete-and I certainly needed one! Thanks a million for it, and for your affectionate birthday message.

With love,
Dorothy

Dear Nance:

I must admit I have a talented sister. The bag is beautiful-and to think you made it yourself! Why, it must have taken **months!**

Thanks, darling-you're an angel to go to so much trouble for me. **I love** the bag, and it goes beautifully with my new brown coat.

Give my love to Fred and the children, and thank them for their birthday wishes. My love to you, **always!**

Dottie

FOR WEDDING ANNIVERSARY GIFTS

The wedding anniversaries that are most frequently celebrated, and for which friends and relatives customarily send gifts, are:

1 year, Paper, Plastics
5 years, Wood
10 years, Tin, Aluminium
15 years, Crystal, Glass
20 years, China
25 years, Silver
30 years, Pearls
35 years,Jade
40 years, Rubies, Garnets
45 years, Sapphires
50 years, Gold
75 years, Diamonds

Such gifts should, of course, be graciously acknowledged by a written note of thanks. The note is written by the wife, for her husband and herself.

Dear Martha:

Jim and I were so touched and pleased that you should have remembered our wedding anniversary! It gave an extra note of happiness to the day.

The **tole** tray is charming; I can hardly wait for an opportunity to use it!

Many thanks to you and Paul for your thoughtful

remembrance, and for your good wishes on our tenth anniversary.

Affectionately,
Harriet

Dear Edna:

How very sweet of you and Dan to remember our anniversary! We were really quite overcome when your package came this morning.

The salad bowl and plates are beautiful. I think they are the loveliest I have ever seen-and so does Ralph.

It's difficult to realize, Edna, that we have been married for twenty years. It certainly doesn't seem that long since I was a bride, and you were my pretty bridesmaid in pink. Remember?

We send you both our love, and our deep appreciation for your thoughts of us on our anniversary. Do come and see us real soon!

Affectionately,
Sally

Dear Carl:

Your flowers came this morning and turned our living room into a garden. Fifty yellow roses for our fifty golden years! How wonderful of you to remember. Carl . . . and so generously!

Steve and I are humble and grateful for our many years of happiness together. And we are grateful, too, for the many good friends we have accumulated along the way. You rank high among them, Carl . . . our dear and loyal friend through all the years.

So we send you our love on our golden anniversary! And we send you our thanks, Carl, for the beautiful roses.

Affectionately,
Lucy

For a Gift for a Newborn Baby

Dear Aunt Ellen:

With all the many things you have to do, how could you find time to make that beautiful sweater and cap set for the baby? I appreciate it twice as much, knowing you made it yourself.

You must come and see my young daughter. George says she's getting real pretty...but of course he's prejudiced, like all fathers. I just think she's **cute**—and very, very precious!

Thanks, Aunt Ellen, for the lovely gift.

Affectionately,
Edith

Dear Mark:

How proud my little Joan will be some day to know that her handsome silver cup came from her godfather.

It's a beautiful gift, Mark . . . and I know Joan will treasure and keep it always, as I have kept my baby cup through all these years.

I hope you know how very much Fred and I appreciate your kindness.

Affectionately yours,
Anne

Ruth, dear:

How like you to be so generous! The quilt is the prettiest one I have ever seen, and just what we needed for Roger's crib.

Why don't you come and see the young fellow? He's really quite a character! I know you are busy during the week—but Sunday afternoon's a good time, and we'd love to see you.

Lou sends his best wishes, and we both send many thanks for the gift.

Affectionately,
Gert

Dear Mrs. Langston:

Thank you ever so much for the beautiful little dress you sent the baby. She wore it home from the hospital, and I just wish you could have seen how sweet she looked in it!

You were very kind to send a gift, and Mr. Cummings and I appreciate it very much. We hope you will come and see the baby now that we are home.

Sincerely yours,
Mary Cummings

FOR A GIFT TO A YOUNG CHILD

Dear Marj:

I just wish you could see how Patsy adores the cute little panda with the big black eyes! I'm sure that if she could write, she'd say, "Thank you, Aunt Marj, for sending me this beautiful panda to love! You are the very best aunt in all the world!"

But little Patsy can't write as yet...so let me thank you for her. You are always so thoughtful and generous.

Come and see us soon, Marj. It's a long time since you have been here.

With love,
Kate

Dear Mrs. Kelly:

Your adorable cap and mitten set came this morning, right on Patsy's birthday. How wonderful of you to remember her!

Thank you very much indeed for Patsy and myself.

Cordially yours,
Katherine Donlin

FOR A HOUSEWARMING GIFT

When you move into a new house and give a party for your friends, they usually bring gifts. And you thank them in person, of course; but that is not enough. You should send an individual note of thanks to each guest who brings something for the new house.

Dear Mary:

I don't know how to thank you for the beautiful cake knife! How did you know it was just what I needed?

John and I appreciate your lovely gift, Mary. We enjoyed seeing you on Friday, and we hope you'll come soon again.

Affectionately,
Alice

Dear Mrs. Hoffman:

Thank you very, very much for the pair of lovely little porcelain vases. John and I think they are simply **beautiful,** and we cannot thank you and Mr. Hoffman enough for them!

The next time you come—which we hope will be very soon-you will see them in all their delicacy and charm occupying a place of honor in our living room.

Cordially yours,
Alice Denton

FOR A BON VOYAGE GIFT

Often when people leave for foreign shores, their relatives and friends, send **bon voyage** gifts to the ship or plane. These may be books, flowers, baskets of fruit ... but whatever they are, each gift should be promptly and cordially acknowledged.

Dear Aunt Jane:

What a precious pair of darlings you and Uncle Ned are to send flowers to our cabin! Jim and I feel like honeymooners instead of a staid old married couple. Our cabin looks just like a bridal suite, with all those wonderful roses you sent us.

Jim and I are very, very happy. We always dreamed of celebrating our fifth anniversary at his home in Scotland, but now that the dream is becoming a reality, we can still hardly believe it!

So far the voyage has been smooth and pleasant, and no one has missed any meals. I certainly hope it continues like this all the way across! We'll write you again as soon as we arrive.

Love from both of us, and many thanks for the flowers!

Yours devotedly,
Gloria

Dear Laura:

It was certainly grand of you and Ted to come and see me off! I know it wasn't easy for you to get to the airport at such an early hour, so I appreciate it all the more.

Flying over water can get dreadfully boring after the first few hours, and your book of detective stories came in very handy. It was sweet and thoughtful of you to think of it.

The flight was uneventful and we arrived in Paris on schedule time. Jeanne and Paul met me at the airport, and we went straight to their charming little house. I know I am going to love it here; I'm looking forward to two **marvelous** weeks with my sister and her husband!

I'll write to you again, Laura. In the meantime, my thanks to you and Ted for your many kindnesses to me—and my love to you both, always!

Blanche

Dear Mr. Peterson.

Your basket of fruit was waiting in my cabin when I got on board this morning. And a more magnificent basket I have never seen!

It was kind and generous of you to do this for me, Mr. Peterson, and I appreciate it more than I can say.

Sincerely yours,
Martha Ellsworth

THE BREAD-AND-BUTTER LETTER

If you have received hospitality at the home of a friend, for a week end or longer, courtesy requires that you write a cordial note of thanks within two or three days after your return home. The fact that you personally and enthusiastically thanked your hostess before leaving doesn't count. You must still express your appreciation **in writing.** This is a so-called "duty" note which is expected of you and which you **must** write. It has become known as a bread-and-butter letter, because it thanks the hostess for the "bread and butter"—or hospitality—she provided.

Kate, dear:

This is to tell you again how very much I enjoyed the week end at Pine Ridge. Everything was just about perfect: the weather, the company, the beautiful surroundings—no wonder I'm finding it difficult to get down to business this morning! The office seems so dull and prosaic after Pine Ridge.

I hope you and Fred know how much I appreciate your hospitality, and your many kindnesses to me. I count myself fortunate indeed to have two such generous and charming friends!

Affectionately yours,
Maureen

Dear Mrs. Franklin:

I'd like you to know how much the week at your lovely house in Southampton has meant to me. I not only enjoyed myself immensely, but I feel relaxed and refreshed as I haven't felt in months!

Please give my love to Betsy. It was so nice being with her again—just like our old days together at school!

Many thanks to you and Mr. Franklin for asking me.

Sincerely yours,
Evelyn McCormack

Dear Mrs. Benton:

Thank you very much for those four wonderful days at Shady Acres! Every moment was a delight, I can't remember ever having enjoyed myself so thoroughly **anywhere!**

It was good of you and Dr. Benton to invite me, and I deeply appreciate your hospitality.

Sincerely yours,
Walter Hanley

THANKS FOR GIFTS TO A PATIENT OR INVALID

If friends send you books, flowers or fruit while you are in the hospital—or ill at home-it is not necessary that you write immediately. But you should write a brief note of thanks as soon as you can, or have someone very close do it for you.

Dear Mr. Martin:

I want to thank you for the beautiful roses you sent Mrs. Granby. She was very happy and pleased when she saw they were from you.

I'm glad to say she is improving rapidly, and I hope she will soon be able to leave the hospital.

We both send you our warmest thanks for the flowers and for your very kind wishes.

Sincerely,
John Granby

Dear George:

It's almost worth being ill to receive such a gorgeous flowers! Your gladioli have certainly transformed this dismal room of mine into a garden. Thank you, George—for the flowers and for your friendly, cheerful note.

They say I may have my first visitors tomorrow and every afternoon thereafter from three to five. I'm glad you want to come and I look forward to seeing you.

Sincerely yours,
Rosalie

Dear Mrs. Thompson:

What a beautiful plant! It is standing on the table right beside my bed, and I'm looking at it-and enjoying it—as I write this note. The gardenia is my favorite flower, and to have a gardenia plant of my own, right at my bedside, is a real treat.

I'm grateful to you for thinking of me in such a lovely way. Thank you, my dear-for the plant, and for being always such a thoughtful and considerate neighbor.

Cordially,
Amy Hackett

Dear Mary and John:

Now that I can finally sit up and write letters, I want to thank you both for the flowers and books you sent me while I was ill—and, most of all, for your many cheerful notes. You have no idea how much they meant to me!

You've been more than kind, you two, and I won't ever forget it. My love and deepest gratitude, now and always!

Jane

THANKS FOR A FAVOR RECEIVED

The gracious person does not accept favors without an expression of thanks and appreciation. Not every favor requires a written note, of course. If you borrow the lawn mower from your neighbor, or ask a friend to send her piano tuner next time he comes-verbal thanks are sufficient. But if a neighbor or friend goes out of the way to do something special for you or a member of your family, nothing but a cordial note of thanks will do to show how grateful you are.

For example, if a friend takes care of your canary while. you are away on a vacation, you thank her in person when you call for your pet ... but you also write a note of thanks:

Dear Lenore:

It was wonderful of you to take such good care or Chipper while we were away. He looked so bright and happy, singing and swinging in the sunshine of your bedroom window, that I felt as though he belonged there and I shouldn't take him back.

I do hope it wasn't too much trouble for you, Lenore. It was certainly a great favor to us, and we want you to know how grateful we are.

Affectionately,
Diane

If a neighbor loans you some expensive or specialized equipment-like a moving-picture camera or a projection machine-you should show your appreciation more tangibly than by your verbal thanks alone. Surely a warm note of thanks is indicated for so generous a favor!

Dear Mr. Rogers:

I am very grateful to you for letting me use your projector last Sunday. Jimmy's birthday party was a huge success because of the movies—and there just wouldn't have been- any movies without your projector!

So I want to thank you most cordially for Jimmy, for his young guests, and for Mrs. Blagdon and myself. We think it was swell of you to be so generous, and we want you to know how very much we all appreciate it.

Sincerely yours,
Hugh R. Blagdon

If a member of your family is visiting in a distant city, and an acquaintance to whom you gave her a letter of introduction is kind and attentive, you naturally write a note of thanks.

Dear Mrs. Hackett:

My niece, Jane Barlow, has written to tell me how very kind you have been to her during her stay in Washington.

Mr. Crawford and I deeply appreciate your courtesy, and we hope to have the opportunity of reciprocating when you are in New York.

With many thanks to you for entertaining Jane so generously.

Sincerely yours,
Margaret F. Crawford

THANKS FOR A LETTER OF CONDOLENCE

Every letter of condolence should be acknowledged by personal note. Commercial "thank you" cards are in bad taste and should be avoided, except in the case of a public official or person of prominence who receives an overwhelming number of letters from strangers. In private life, sending an engraved form of thanks to a friend or acquaintance who has expressed sympathy is looked upon as rude and ungracious.

The reply to a note of sympathy or condolence need not be written as promptly as other notes of thanks. It can he mailed any time within six weeks after receipt of the flowers or note of sympathy. It can be brief to the point of saying nothing more than a simple "Thank you for your kind expression of sympathy." Or it can be as wordy as one's feelings and impulses at the time prompt. To an intimate friend, for example, one might write:

Dear Anne:

I shall always remember with gratitude the letter you wrote me when you learned of Claire's death. No one but you, who knew my sister and loved her as her own family did, could have written that letter. It brought me comfort, Anne, at a time when I needed it badly.

Thank you from the bottom of my heart, for your letter and for your many kindnesses to Claire during her long illness.

Affectionately,
Carol

To a friend who has asked in her note of sympathy if she can help in any way, one might reply:

Dear Ida:

Thank you for your kind note of sympathy, and for your offer to help.

I'm afraid there's nothing anyone can do to help us right now. Only time can help us get over the terrible shock of Philip's death.

But it was good of you to make the offer, and I appreciate it more than I can say.

Always affectionately,
Gail

A woman who has lost her husband may find it difficult to write notes of thanks even to her most intimate friends. She may ask a son or daughter, or some other close relative, to acknowledge the flowers and the letters of condolence she received.

Dear Mrs. Hartley:

Mother has asked me to write to you, as she cannot do so herself just now.

She would like you and Mr. Hartley to know how much she appreciates the flowers and the letter of sympathy you sent. You have both been very kind.

Sincerely yours,
Virginia Baxter

This is the type of letter one generally writes to a neighbor who has sent flowers and made a call of condolence:

Dear Mrs. Davis:

You were very kind at the time of my mother's death. I want you to know how much your sympathy and thoughtfulness have meant to me, and how grateful I am for all you did.

With heartfelt thanks,

Sincerely yours,
Thelma Conners

A girl called home from college by the death of her father, might receive flowers and a note from her classmates. She would write a note to the girl closest to her at school, asking her to thank the others for their expression of sympathy.

Dear Grace:

The letter and the flowers came on Tuesday. Will you please give my thanks to all the girls, and tell them how much mother and I appreciate their thoughtfulness?

I shall try to return to school on Tuesday if mother is feeling well enough by that time.

With affection,
Annette

A difficult note of thanks is the one a man writes at the time of his wife's death to friends they have known intimately for many years, and with whom they have shared many happy experiences.

Dear Kate:

I don't need to tell you and Paul how greatly I appreciate all you have done for me in these trying weeks—and how grateful I am for the comfort and understanding you gave me when I needed them so desperately.

No one knows better than you two what Christine meant to me, and what an aching void my life has become without her. But I am trying to take your advice, Kate- and I hope that returning to my work next week will help fill some of the emptiness.

You and Paul have been splendid. I really don't know what I would have done without you. Thank you for everything.

Affectionately,
Todd

THANKS FOR A LETTER OF CONGRATULATION

When friends take the trouble to write and congratulate you on your birthday or anniversary, on your engagement or marriage, on a talk you gave, a prize you won, or a distinction you earned . . . you owe them a gracious note of thanks in acknowledgment. Whether it's a brief and formal note, or a long and newsy letter, depends upon the circumstances and upon the degree of intimacy with your correspondent. Here, for example, are two notes of thanks for birthday congratulations:

Dear Mrs. Martin:

I just can't tell you how flattered I am that you should have remembered my birthday. It was a real pleasure to receive your charming note this morning.

Thank you so much for your good wishes!

Sincerely yours,
Hilda Rankin

Florence, dear:

What do you mean by "congratulations"? Why should I be congratulated for being a year older?

But thanks for remembering my birthday ... and for your simply **priceless** letter! I can't remember when I enjoyed a letter as much, Florence. It was just as though you were right here in the room with me, laughing and talking.

Which reminds me—when are you going to pay us that visit you promised? We've had our living room completely redecorated since you were here last Spring, and I'd like you to see it. Furthermore, Tom has some new home movies he enjoys showing off, so come real soon and make the guy happy! I must admit the movies are quite good—almost professional.

It was grand hearing from you, and I'm so glad to know little Dan is better and back at school. Give him my love, and tell him I haven't forgotten that he wants a pup from Nellie's next batch. But Nellie seems to be taking her time!

Our best to you and Bill, and **do** drive out soon to see us!

Always affectionately,
Doris

Announcement of an engagement is generally followed by letters of congratulation and good wishes from relatives and friends. Such letters should be acknowledged by a personal note of thanks. A letter of congratulation addressed to the young lady is answered by her; a letter to her fiance is answered by him:

Dear Aunt Emma:

It was sweet of you to write. Thanks very much for your good wishes.

I'm sure you'll like Alan. He's a grand person, and no one can help liking him! We promise to come and see you and Uncle Fred real soon.

With love,
Judy

Dear Louise:

What a wonderful letter! Thanks so much for your good wishes, and for all the nice things you wrote about Alan and me.

I guess I'm just about the happiest girl in the world, Louise. I know now what you meant when you said you and Phil were made for each other. I feel the same way about Alan!

Thanks again for your letter. If the future holds only half the fine things you hope for us, we'll be lucky indeed!

Affectionately,
Judy

Dear Aunt Mary:

I'm glad you and Uncle John approve so heartily of my engagement. I knew you would love Judy—everyone does. She's everything you say in your letter-and more! I'm a lucky fellow to have won such a grand girl.

Thanks for writing. I hope to deserve all the happiness and good things in life you wish for me.

Affectionately,
Alan

Dear Tom:

You're right! Judy's the cream of the crop and I'm the luckiest fellow in the world!

Thanks so much for your letter. Judy and I appreciate your congratulations and good wishes.

Sincerely,
Alan

Announcement of a marriage is also generally followed by letters of congratulation and good wishes. These, too, should be acknowledged by personal notes of thanks ... **never** by printed or engraved "thank you" cards.

Dear Mrs. Snowden:

Thank you ever so much for your charming note of congratulation. My nice new husband and I appreciate your letter, and your good wishes for the future.

We will be at home after November first, and we hope you will come and see how cozy we are in our little apartment.

Cordially yours,
Judith T. Powell

Dearest Elaine:

Of all the letters Alan and I have received since our marriage, we enjoyed yours the most! Thank you, darling, for all those good wishes. If our life together proves half as rosy as you predict, we'll be well content!

You say Alan is to be congratulated, but I think I'm to be congratulated, too. He's a wonderful, wonderful husband, Elaine, and I just can't tell you how happy I am!

Thanks again for your good wishes. Alan joins me in hoping you'll come often to see us in Garden City.

With affectionate greetings from us both,

Judy

ACKNOWLEDGING VARIOUS OTHER NOTES OF CONGRATULATION

People who are generous and kindly like to acknowledge every message of congratulation, even though a note of thanks may not actually be required. For example, there is no rule that says you must acknowledge every birthday greeting, every anniversary card, every letter of congratulation on winning, a prize or receiving an honor or distinction. But such letters deserve acknowledgment; and the people who write them always enjoy and appreciate a note of thanks in response. It can be a very short note, just a few words or a single brief paragraph; but it should be friendly and sincere.

On a Wedding Anniversary

Dear Cynthia:

Your letter took us back twenty years, and brought so many happy memories to mind! Thank you, dear, for remembering our anniversary and for your kind thoughts of us. Paul joins me in sending our love and appreciation.

Affectionately,
Janice

On the Birth of a Child

Dear Mrs. Hanson:

What a lot of fine big wishes you made for our very tiny new daughter! Thank you ever so much-for Mr. Bradley and myself. We deeply appreciate your good wishes and congratulations.

Sincerely yours,
Vera Bradley

On Graduating from College

Dear Mrs. Kellogg:

Your letter was a pleasant surprise. Thank you so much

for your congratulations and good wishes

I have no immediate plans for the future, but I hope to make advertising my career.

Please remember me to Mr. Kellogg, and tell him I appreciate his good wishes for my future.

Sincerely yours,
Gertrude Hill

Dear Mr. Kimball:

That was a wonderful letter you wrote me! I certainly appreciate your congratulations, and your invitation to come and see you about a job.

But as Dad must have told you by now, I am interested in industrial design and hope to find an opening in that field.

It's quite an exciting adventure, starting out in the business world—and I guess I'll need all the good wishes my friends have been sending me!

Thanks ever so much for your interest, Mr. Kimball, and for your very kind offer.

Sincerely yours,
Edwin Halleck

On Winning a Prize

Dear Mrs. Loomis:

I assure you I was very much surprised when my poster won! Thank you for your congratulations, and for your kind comments about my work.

Sincerely,
Evelyn Palmer

Dear Jeff:

One of the nicest things about winning the interstate debating contest was getting all those wonderful letters from my friends.

It sure was great hearing from you, Jeff. I'm glad to know you have finally decided on medicine; I always said you'd make a swell doctor!

Thanks a lot for the congratulations. I guess I was just lucky.

My kindest regards to your parents,

Cordially,
Al Fisher

On Winning an Honor or Distinction

Dear Mrs. Dwight:

I am humble and grateful for the distinction of being named outstanding mother of Middletown. Nothing could have pleased me more!

Many thanks to you and Mr. Dwight for your kind note of congratulation.

Sincerely yours,
Julia L. Marlowe

Dear Dr. Benton:

Thank you very much for your note of congratulation on my election as president of the state medical association.

It was good of you to take the time and trouble to write, and I sincerely appreciate your kindness.

Cordially yours,
Frederick P. Harmon, M.D.

On Publication of a Book

Dear Miss Halloway:

What a pleasant surprise to hear from you after all these years!

I am glad you like my new book, and I appreciate your good wishes for its success.

Thank you very much indeed for writing.

Sincerely yours,
Lillian E. Watson

Bear in mind that any thoughtful complimentary attention requires an appreciative note in response. If someone congratulates you on a talk you made, a paper you read, a concert you gave, a painting or photograph you exhibited, write a brief of thanks. It takes only a moment, but it helps widen immeasurably your sphere of friendly influence and affection.

❑ ❑ ❑ ❑ ❑

Chapter VIII

LETTERS OF CONGRATULATION

IF you hear of a friend's engagement or marriage, if you hear of the birth of a child or of an honor or distinction that has come to someone you know-sit down right away, while you are elated and excited by the news, and write a letter of congratulation. Sincerity comes more easily and naturally to your written words at such a time, and your note has a truer ring to it.

So never put off any letter of congratulation that needs to be written. Don't he satisfied to write it in your thoughts, promising yourself to put it on paper at the first opportunity. Write it while the news is still fresh in your mind! You'll find that it pays to keep up with your correspondence. You'll find that all your letters of thanks, of sympathy, of congratulation are much easier to write if you write them on time.

Letters of congratulation should be especially easy and pleasant to write, for we all like to share in the joy of some happy event. These are cheerful messages, in which you can spread yourself to your heart's content. The note may be brief and formal, or it may be chatty and informal—depending on the circumstances. The important thing is that it be sincere. The desire to congratulate should be clearly present.

Cultivate the habit of writing notes of congratulation even when they are not actually required of you-to friends who have graduated or been promoted, who have had a birthday or anniversary, or any other occasion that warrants a complimentary message. It's a very charming habit to have, and one that cannot fail to make you more popular with your family and friends. A little note of congratulation can give a big lift, and is often remembered a lifetime with pleasure and appreciation.

CONGRATULATIONS ON AN ENGAGEMENT

Always be sure that the **occasion** for congratulation is mentioned specifically in your letter. Don't write "I've heard the news and hasten to congratulate you" but "I've heard the news of your engagement and hasten to congratulate you."

A young lady is not customarily congratulated either on her engagement or her wedding. It's the man who congratulated; the lady is sent good wishes for her happiness.

Dear Lenore:

I have just learned of your engagement to Shelley Travers. Let me be among the first to wish you both every happiness.

I've known Shelley for years, and I'm very fond of the lad. But I think he's lucky to have won a grand girl like you; and tell him for me, my dear, that I congratulate him!

Affectionately,
Hilda K. Brandon

Dear Lenore:

What exciting news! I'm delighted to hear of your engagement, and I wish you all the happiness in the world.

I don't know your Mr. Travers, but I'm anxious to meet him. I'm sure he must be someone special to have won your heart.

I hope you will both be very happy, always!

Fondly,
Janet

Dearest Lenore:

Your mother has told us of your engagement to Shelley Travers. I can't tell you, my dear, how pleased your Uncle Fred and I are by this news. We have been very close to Shelley's family for years, as you know—and we have always thought of him as an unusually fine and dependable young man. In fact, we don't know anyone we would rather have you marry than him!

So we send you our love, Lenore—and our wishes for a lifetime of happiness. Give Shelley our love too, and tell him how delighted we are to welcome him into the family.

Always affectionately,
Aunt May

Dear Lenore:

I can't say that Bill and I were exactly surprised by the news of your engagement to Shelley. We've been rather expecting it right along.

We think it's simply **swell**, of course. We never knew two people more suited to each other (except ourselves!).

But seriously, Lenore, Bill and I are very glad for you, as we know how happy you must be. We send congratulations to you **both**; and we wish you every good fortune and every possible happiness in your life together.

Lovingly,
Pat

Dear Miss Bailey:

I have just learned of your engagement to Shelley Travers. He's a fine chap, and a very lucky one! Please give him my congratulations. I hope you will both be very happy.

Sincerely yours,
Milton Ames

Dear Shelley:

That's great news about you and Lenore! She's a wonderful girl in every way, and we congratulate you on your good fortune.

Best wishes from us both on your engagement. We hope you will have nothing but joy and happiness in your life together.

Affectionately,
Ethel and George

Dear Shelley:

I just can't tell you, Shelley, how pleased I am by the announcement of your engagement. From what I hear of the young lady, she is charming and very lovely—and will make you an excellent wife.

Your Aunt Charlotte and I send congratulations, and best wishes for your happiness. We hope you'll bring the young lady here soon so that we can meet her. Please give her our affectionate regards, and tell her she has every good wish from us both.

Fondly,
Uncle Matt

Dear Shelley:

I know how crazy you've always been about that precious Lenore of yours; and from what you've told me about her, she's something to be crazy about! So I guess you're a pretty lucky fellow, and I congratulate you.

Some day I hope to meet Lenore. In the meantime, tell her your old pal sends his best wishes for her happiness. And that goes for you, too!

As ever,
Bob

CONGRATULATIONS ON MARRIAGE

When an announcement of a marriage is received, congratulations are usually sent to the bride and groom. Ale note is customarily written and addressed to both; but it may also be written to the bride individually, or to the groom individually—as indicated in the various examples below.

Dear Anne and Jerry:

We were thrilled and delighted to receive the announcement of your marriage in Springtown last Tuesday.

Tom and I send you both our love, and best wishes for every happiness that life can bring.

We hope you'll let us know when you return to New York, so that we can give you our congratulations in person.

Affectionately,
Barbara

Dear Anne:

I was pleasantly surprised to receive the announcement of your marriage in this morning's mail.

I hope you will be very happy. Congratulations to Mr. Carter, and my very best wishes to both of you for happiness and everything good in life.

Sincerely,
Katherine Miller

Dear Mrs. Carter,

Let me wish you and Mr. Carter every happiness on your recent marriage.

With best wishes from Mr. Millen and myself.

Sincerely yours,
Sarah G. Millen

Dear Anne:

You will always be little Anne to me . . . even though

you're now a staid and dignified married woman! It's hard for me to believe you are old enough to be married. Why, it seems only yesterday I dangled you on my knee!

Give my congratulations to that nice new husband of yours, and tell him I think he's a mighty lucky fellow.

My very best wishes to you, for a lifetime of happiness.

Affectionately,
Wilbur T. Ross

Anne, dear:

So you and Jerry are married! You've certainly taken all your friends by surprise. But I think you were wise to eliminate a long engagement. It's just what I would have done in your place!

Jerry's a grand fellow, and I know you'll always be very happy. Are you getting used to having people call you "Mrs. Carter" as yet?

I'd love, to hear all about the wedding. Write and tell me, when you can. In the meantime, I send you my love and best wishes . . . and I hope you and Jerry have a long, happy life together!

Fondly,
Cynthia

Dear Jerry:

I've just returned from California—to find the announcement of your marriage waiting for me. Congratulations, old boy! I certainly wish you every happiness.

I haven't had the pleasure of meeting the lady of your choice, but from what I hear she must be wonderful. Please tell her, your old friend Jim Colton sends good wishes, and hopes she'll always be as happy as she is right now. I look forward to the pleasure of meeting her soon.

The best of everything to both of you!

Cordially,
Jim

My dear Carter:

Congratulations on your recent marriage.

I wish you and your bride the best of luck, and ever increasing happiness as the years go by.

Sincerely yours,
Robert F. Wheeler

CONGRATULATIONS ON A WEDDING ANNIVERSARY

Dear Harriet:

It doesn't seem possible that it's five years since you and Bob were married! Somehow I still think of you as a bride and groom. Maybe it's because you're just about the most devoted couple I know!

Congratulations to you both, and may the years ahead bring you continued joy and contentment.

Affectionately,
Janice

Dear Helen and Fred:

I looked at the calendar yesterday and suddenly realized it's your tenth anniversary! My, how the years fly by!

Ralph and I send you congratulations, an every best wish for the future. We hope you'll have many, many more anniversaries—each one happier than the last.

I wonder if you know what an inspiration your sweet devotion to each other has always been to your friends?

Always affectionately,
Lillian

Dear Mrs. Dearing:

We have heard that you and Mr. Dearing are celebrating your fiftieth wedding anniversary this week.

It must be a great source of pleasure and pride to have reached this milestone in your long and happy life together, and to be able to look back upon a rich and full life and know you have accumulated so many devoted friends.

Mr. Phillips and I send you warm congratulations and we hope that there are many more years of happiness ahead for both of you.

Cordially yours,
Myra L. Phillips

CONGRATULATIONS ON A BIRTHDAY

Birthday cards are universally used, and there is no real objection to them. At least they show you have not forgotten the day. But a written message, no matter how short, always means twice as much-and especially on a birthday. A few words in your own handwriting have far more meaning and sincerity than the most eloquent sentiment ever printed on a card. So if you have real affection for your relatives and friends, write them personal notes of congratulation instead of sending ready-made congratulations printed on a card.

Jane, dear:

You may not like to be reminded that you are a year older today—but that's not going to keep me from saying "Happy Birthday!"

Let's see.... Is it twenty-seven, or twenty-eight—? Or perhaps I'd better not ask!

Anyway, my love to you on your birthday, Jane and many, many happy returns of the day! Next time you come into town to do some shopping, call me and I'll meet you for lunch.. It's been too long since we had one of our good old-fashioned chats!

Affectionately,
Sonya

Dear Aunt Agatha:

Today is your birthday, and I'm thinking of you and wondering how you are. Have you been well this past month? Hasn't the weather been simply **frightful?**

It's too bad you live so far away, Aunt Agatha. If you only lived a little closer, I could come and say "Happy Birthday" to you in person. But as it is, all I can do is the next best thing: send you my love, my congratulations and my very best wishes for the coming year!

So you see my thoughts are right there in Glencove with you, even though I am not!

Lovingly,
Margaret

Dearest Judy:

Is it really your birthday again? Where do the years fly so swiftly? But I'm sure **you** don't mind! **The** years never show on you, Judy.... Why, you look younger today than when I first met you more than ten year ago!

But I didn't write this letter to pay you compliments! I wrote to tell you I'm thinking of you on your birthday, and wishing you everything your heart desires in the year ahead. Congratulations, Judy dear-and many.. many happy returns of the day!

With affection
Elaine

Dear Dick:

A little bird told me it's your birthday. So I'm sending

congratulations and my very best wishes—for now and all your birthdays to come!

Sincerely,
Mary Lou

Dear Uncle John:

To everybody else in the world, this may be Columbus Day. But to me it's a far more special day than that! It's the birthday of my favorite uncle-the uncle who never ever forgot my birthday when I was a child and who always made me so happy!

I wish you weren't way out there in Highbridge, Uncle John. I'd love to see you on your birthday and help you celebrate. But I can't—so I'm sending you a little gift I hope you'll like. With it go my congratulations, and all my love. I hope you'll have many, many happy birthdays, and that you'll' never lose the cheerful outlook and gay spirits that have made you so well loved by all the family.

Bill and the children join me in sending congratulations. Love from all of us.

Cornelia

A letter like the above is bound to make a lonely old man, living far away, feel much happier on his birthday than any printed card-however beautiful its decorations or sentimental its verses!

Here is a suitable birthday note for a young man to send a girl he doesn't know very well:

Dear Miss Heller:

My sister tells me this is your birthday. Please accept my heartiest congratulations. I hope you'll enjoy many, many birthdays—and that each one finds you happier than the one before.

Sincerely yours,
Harold Riker

To someone he knows well, he would naturally write a more informal and spontaneous note of congratulation:

Dear Babs:

So you're a year older today—or don't you want to be reminded? Anyway, congratulations and best wishes and all that sort of thing.

If you feel in the mood for celebrating, will you let me take you the dinner and the movies, as a sort of birthday treat? You name the day. And in the meantime, many happy returns!

Cordially,
Harold

CONGRATULATIONS ON THE BIRTH OF A CHILD

Everybody's happy when a baby is born. To express your pleasure and share in the joy, you write the proud new mother a note of congratulation.

Dear Helen:

Mother just phoned and told me the wonderful news. You and Phil have a baby boy! I'm so happy and excited, you'd think it were my baby instead of yours!

Congratulations, darling . . . and may you never have anything but happiness from your son. He can't help being fine and splendid in every way, with you and Phil for parents.

My love to you both-you proud and happy parents!—and to that little fellow who just arrived. I'm coming to see him as soon as I know I won't be in the way.

Affectionately,
Winifred

Marjorle, dear:

What wonderful news! I know you wanted a baby girl—I can just imagine how thrilled and happy you must be.

Dan must be just bursting with pride. Tell him that Carl and I send congratulations and best wishes-and that goes **double** for you, Marj!

We wish you both all possible joy and happiness in your new little daughter.

Fondly,
Claire

A letter of congratulation on the birth of a child should not be facetious unless written by a close friend or a member of the family. Here, for example, is a letter that a friendly good-natured young woman might write to a cousin with whom she has always maintained a close relationship:

Dearest Fran:

All the raves I've been hearing about a certain young person, recently arrived, makes me a bit skeptical. I just don't believe a mite of a baby girl, less than a week old, can be so beautiful. I simply can't believe she has all the marvelous qualities everyone says she has!

Seeing's believing—so when can I come and see this amazing small person for myself? Will you have Jim phone and let me know?

In the meantime, congratulations to both of you and all my love!

Nancy

A letter of congratulation on a new baby, from a male member of the family, should be cordial and gay . . . and a bit on the flattering side:

Dear Marjorie:

Congratulations on the new baby! I hear she is simply beautiful, even at five days old. But she'll have to go a long way to be even half as lovely as her mothers!

Bill tells me you are calling her Marianne. It's a charming name....

Hurry and get well so that I can come and see you, and judge for myself whether little Marianne is as beautiful as they say.

Affectionately,
Edgar

Here is the kind of letter a woman might write to a neighbor who has had a new baby:

Dear Mrs. Harper:

Your husband just told me the good news. I'm so glad to hear it's a boy, for now little Barbam will have that baby brother she's been wanting!

Congratulations from Mr. Martin and myself. We wish you joy and happiness with your son.

Sincerely yours,
Nellie Martin

Letters are not generally sent to the father, though an intimate friend may want to send a note like the following:

Dear Phil:

So it's a boy! My heartiest congratulations to you and Marjorie. And my best wishes for everything fine and good in life for the little fellow.

I'll come and see Marjorie and the baby when they are home from the hospital.

Sincerely,
Ken

CONGRATULATIONS ON GRADUATION

Dear John:

Congratulations upon having received your doctorate in philosophy from Princeton University. I know this has meant years of study and hard work on your part, and it's an achievement you can well be proud of.

Your Aunt Emma and I have followed your progress with pleasure and interest; and we are sure, from the fine record you have made, that you will be a success in whatever you undertake.

No doubt you are tired after the strain of the past few months; and if you would like to come to Lake Talbot for a few weeks this summer, we'd be very happy to have you. We remember that you always used to like it here as a boy; and although it may be too quiet for you now, the rest and relaxation might do you a lot of good. And we'd certainly enjoy hearing about your plans, now that you have completed your college course.

Think it over, John, and let us know.

Affectionately,
Uncle Clint

Dear John:

I have just learned of your graduation from Princeton.

Please accept my heartiest congratulations, and best wishes for your future success.

Sincerely yours,
Harriet Cranford

Dear John:

Bill tells me you have successfully completed your course at Princeton and have received your doctorate in philosophy. He's very proud of his big brother, and I can't say I blame him! You've made a fine record, and all your old friends back here in Middletown are proud of you.

I understand you'll be here for a few weeks this summer before going to your uncle's place in the mountains. I am looking forward to seeing you and hearing about your plans for the future.

In the meantime, congratulations and best wishes to you, John!

Cordially,
Alice

Dear Mrs. Malcolm:

We hear that John has graduated from Princeton and that he made a very fine record for himself there. You must be proud of his splendid accomplishment, and we are very happy for you.

Please give John our congratulations, and our best wishes for success and happiness in his chosen work.

Sincerely yours,
Myra T. Clark

Dearest Mary:

It doesn't seem possible that you are grown up—and a graduate of Vassar! It was such a little while ago that you used to come and visit me, just so you could swing on my garden gate. Remember?

I'm very proud of you, Mary dear. I've heard all about your fine achievements at college. Just saying "Congratulations" doesn't seem enough; so I'm sending you a gift that I hope you like and find useful. With it goes my love, and my hopes for your happiness and success in the interesting career you have selected.

Devotedly,
Aunt Jean

Dear Miss Abbott:

May I join in the chorus of friendly congratulations that you must be receiving from all sides today on your graduation from Vassar?

Your parents have told me how brilliantly you have distinguished yourself this past year, and how many honors you have won. They are very proud of you, as they well may be. I'm proud of you, too-and I'm just an old neighbor and friend!

I understand you are going to Chicago to join the editorial staff of a new teen-age magazine. My best wishes go with you, my dear! I know it's the work you love and what you have always wanted to do. I'm sure you'll be a great success.

The best of luck to you!

Cordially,
Marion G. Hazlitt

Dear Mary:

I have just learned of your graduation from Vassar, and your plans to go to Chicago to take an editorial job.

May an old friend congratulate you, and wish you the very best of success?

Sincerely,
Bob Traymore

Dear Mary:

First let me congratulate you on your graduation from Vassar. You certainly distinguished yourself, from what I hear!

Then let me congratulate you on that swell job you got in Chicago. Isn't it **wonderful** to get just exactly the kind of job you've been wanting and hoping for! But you deserve it, Mary—and I'm sure this is the beginning of a very brilliant and successful career for you.

I know you'll be very busy, but I hope you'll find time to write now and then and let me know how you are getting along. I don't need to tell you how interested I am!

With every good wish for the future,

Affectionately,
Carolyn

CONGRATULATIONS ON WINNING AN HONOR OR DISTINCTION

Dear Mrs. Marlowe:

It gave me the greatest possible pleasure to learn that you were named Middletown's outstanding mother of the year. I know of no one who deserves this great distinction more than you.

Congratulations from Mr. Dwight and myself. All your old neighbors and friends are very proud of you!

Cordially yours,
Jennie T. Dwight

Dear Dr. Harmon:

My warm congratulations to you on your election as president of the state medical association. It's a fine tribute from your colleagues, and a reward you richly deserve for your many years of splendid service to the profession and to the people of the state.

I can't think of any man who would have been a better choice. My very best wishes to you!

Sincerely yours,
Thomas M. Benton, M.D.

CONGRATULATIONS ON A PROMOTION OR A NEW VENTURE

Dear Mr. Forthright:

I read in this morning's paper that after twenty-five years with Courtway and Pratt, you are branching out for yourself and opening your own advertising agency.

I would like to add my congratulations to the many you must be receiving. With your brilliant background and long record of fine achievements, I'm sure the new agency will be a great success. I sincerely hope you will find in this new venture the happiness and satisfaction you so richly deserve.

Cordially yours,
Lillian E. Watson

Dear Al:

I ran into Carl the other day, and he tells me you were recently appointed managing editor of the Middle town **Star.**

It's great news, Al-and I'm delighted to hear it! I knew it would be only a matter of time before your unusual abilities were recognized.

It's fine to know you have achieved the goal you've been working toward all these years, and I wish you the greatest possible success. In my opinion, the **Star** at last has an editor who can make it the dominant, outstanding daily of the Middle West!

My heartiest congratulations!

Sincerely yours,
Bert Fellows

Dear Jim:

Congratulations on the opening of the Middletown Clinic! We know it represents the dream of a lifetime, and we're so very happy that your dream has at last become a reality.

The institution will perform a great service to the people; and under your capable guidance, it cannot fail to be a credit to the community.

Paul and I send our very best wishes to you and to the members of your staff.

Affectionately,
Helen Lawson

CONGRATULATIONS ON WINNING A PRIZE

Dear Mrs. Palmer:

Imagine my delight to read in this morning's paper that you had won first prize in the poster contest! I didn't know we had such a talented neighbor.

Congratulations! I think your poster is *marvelous*; I've clipped it out of the paper so I can show it to all my friends.

Sincerely yours,
Jennifer Loomis

Dear Walter:

Your mother tells me you have won the singles championship and that you now rank third among the top boy players in the country. I'm sure you must be very happy and proud.

Congratulations from Mr. Clinton and myself, and keep up the good work!

Sincerely yours,
Sarah Clinton

CONGRATULATIONS ON A SPEECH OR A PERFORMANCE

Dear Roger:

I simply **glow** with admiration when I think of the wonderful speech you made last night at town hall, We have all long been aware of the alarming increase in juvenile delinquency here in Middletown. But no one has ever had the courage to place the blame squarely where it belongs . . . as you did last night.

Congratulations on a brilliant and forceful speech! I'm sure that all the mothers who heard it must be as delighted and as grateful as I am. It's bound to do a lot of good.

Cordially,
Nancy Evans

Dear Miss Vuillimet:

Congratulations on your triumph last night! Everybody in Middletown is talking about your brilliant piano recital.

Mother and I are especially fond of the Tchaikovsky Concerto, and your rendition of it was simply **superb**. I just can't tell you how", much we enjoyed it!

Sincerely yours,
Fredericka Hollings

Dear Bill:

I attended the track meet yesterday and I saw you win the 100-yard dash. It was a splendid performance, and I congratulate you! Keep up that kind of running and you'll make the next Olympic team!

Sincerely,
Ted Baxter

❐ ❐ ❐ ❐ ❐

Chapter IX

LETTERS OF CONDOLENCE

AMONG the most difficult letters of all to write are letters of condolence. Many people find them so difficult that they send telegrams, printed cards, flowers-anything to avoid writing a personal note of sympathy!

And yet, there is probably no time when a letter can mean so much and be so deeply appreciated. It always helps to know that friends are sympathetic and understanding. A few sincere, well-chosen words can give comfort even to the most grief-stricken . . . can renew the faith and courage of those cruelly hurt and embittered by their loss.

So even though you send flowers or make a condolence call, always write a letter as well to any relative or friend who has suffered a bereavement. Put your sympathy and understanding on paper—**write down** the way you feel—for the greater comfort such written words can give.

A good letter of condolence is like a handclasp, warm and friendly. It is written with dignity and restraint, not filled with gushy sentiment. It's brief, for this is no time to be wordy. It says only what you truly feel: that and nothing more. It doesn't dwell on details of the illness or death, nor quote "comforting" passages from poetry, or the Bible. It doesn't touch on memories that reopen the floodgates of pain and sorrow.

Often, in a note of condolence, it's not so much what you say as what you don't say that counts. Surely there can be neither comfort nor compassion in a letter that says, "She was too young to die! " or "Your life will be desolate without him! " It's better not to write at all than to write so tactlessly. A letter of condolence is written for one purpose only: **to**

give comfort. And it cannot give comfort if it's tactless, or thoughtless or very obviously insincere.

It shouldn't be difficult to write a good letter of condolence if you are genuinely moved to sympathy by a friend's misfortune. It shouldn't be difficult to write with kindness and understanding if you feel that friend's grief and share in the tragic impact of it. The important thing is to write promptly, as soon as you hear the news and before the shock of it has worn off. For if you write while your heart is filled with sadness, your letter will have the ring of sincerity to it. You letter will be a warm and convincing expression of the sympathy you really feel.

When you sit down to write a note of condolence, don't think about the right words and phrases to use. Don't strive for eloquence and effect. Remember, it's the feeling behind the words that counts, not the words themselves. Think of the person who is gone. Think of the heartache and sorrow of the person to whom you are writing. Put down simply and truthfully what you think and feel at that moment. Never mind the words. Write what's in your heart . . . and the words will come without coaxing.

Just remember that the three most essential qualities of a good condolence letter are **tact, sincerity** and **brevity.** A single sentence that expresses real feeling is better than a whole page of meaningless and insincere eloquence.

Following are examples of condolence letters representing a wide range of circumstances. These are not intended as set forms, to be used word for word; but as models or patterns to help you write comforting and understanding messages of your own.

ON THE DEATH OF A PARENT

Dear Margaret:

News has just come to me of your great loss. I cannot

tell you how shocked and grieved I am. I wish I could be with you and comfort you in your sorrow.

I know how you adored your mother. It should be a great comfort to you now to know that you were always so very good and kind to her. Everyone says you were the most wonderful daughter a mother ever had! So don't grieve, my dear; she wouldn't want you to.

You have my love, and my heartfelt sympathy.

Affectionately,
Anne

Dear Margaret:

I want you to know how much I sympathize with you and your family.

Long after today's grief shall pass away, as fortunately it must, you will have as a consoling memory the knowledge of all that you meant and were to your mother. We all know of your unfailing devotion, and cherish and admire you for it.

My thoughts are with you now, and I send you my deepest sympathy.

Affectionately yours,
Edgar Tyler

Margaret, dear:

If only I knew what to say to comfort you! But words cannot say what is in my heart, nor tell you how deeply I feel for you in your sorrow.

I loved your mother, too, Margaret, and I'll never get over missing her. You know I share your grief, but how I wish that sharing it could lighten the burden for you!

I send you all my love, darling, and all my sympathy,

Devotedly,
Jane

Dear Margaret:

I know words aren't much comfort at a time like this. But I'd like you to know I'm thinking of you; and that my family and I send our heartfelt sympathy.

Sincerely,
Jim

Dear Margaret:

Today I heard you had lost your mother. I know the suddenness of it must have been a dreadful shock, and I just can't tell you how sorry I am. Having been so recently through the same sad experience, I know only too well what it means....

I wish there were something I could do or say to soften your grief. But only time can do that, Margaret—and it **will**, as surely as it did for me.

With deepest sympathy to you and all your family,

Affectionately,
Vera T. Hubbard

Dearest Margaret:

I'm sorry to be so far away when you need me. . . . Just be the fine, brave person you have always been. You had your mother with you for many happy years, Margaret, and as time goes on you will find comfort, and peace in your beautiful memories of her.

I'll hurry back to New York as soon as I can. In the meantime, I send you my love—and I hope you will turn to me for any help or comfort I can give, now and always.

Your devoted,
Aunt Kate

Dear Miss Conners:

We know how much your mother meant to you and how great your sorrow must be. We sincerely wish we could help share your burden until it gets lighter.

Mr. Burke joins me in sending heartfelt condolences to you and your family.

Cordially yours,
Mary G. Burke

Dear Miss Conners:

Please accept my very deepest sympathy on the death of your mother.

I can well appreciate what a great loss this must be to you.

Sincerely yours,
Frederick T. Warner

Dear Miss Conners:

We have heard the sad news and hasten to offer you our sympathy.

We hope you will call on us if there is anything we can do to help.

Sincerely,
Ellen and Joe Hartley

Dear Paul:

I cannot tell you how shocked I was to hear of your sudden great loss. Everyone who knew your mother loved and admired her.

I wish there were something I could do to help you in your grief; but all I can do is send you my very deepest sympathy.

Affectionately,
Grace

Dear Paul:

I've just heard the sad news, and I hasten to Offer my sympathy.

Please call on me if there is anything I can do to help.

Sincerely,
Bob

Dear Paul:

I feel it's almost an intrusion to write at a time like this. But I must tell you how saddened we are by the news, and how deeply we feel for you in your sorrow. It was a privilege to have known your mother; and her loss will be felt by many, for a long time to come.

Fred and I hope that time will quickly soften the blow, and leave you only cherished memories.

Affectionately,
Mary Haskins

Dear Paul:

Your sorrow is shared by everyone who knew and loved your mother. There's little I can say, except that your grief is mine—and I only wish I could take away some part of it.

Affectionately,
Amy

Dear Paul:

Your wonderful mother—my sister—is gone. I know what your grief must be, for I know well what she always meant to you, and how completely devoted you were to each other.

I can't tell you how sorry I am that a continent now separates us. I'd like to be with you, Paul, and I'm distressed by the circumstances which make it impossible for me to fly to New York.

But I'm with you in thought, my boy. And although I share your grief, I urge you to find solace in the realization that you were all and everything to your mother . . . you made her so happy and proud! Everyone knows what a fine son you always were, in every way.

So try not to grieve too much, Paul. Try to believe as I do: that your mother is still right there with you, and that she will keep on being proud of you and your work.

Your aunt sends her love and deepest sympathy. We both hope you can arrange to spend a little time with us soon in Los Angeles. And I do hope, Paul, you will always count me a loyal and devoted friend, as well as your affectionate.

Uncle Dave

Dear Mr. Owen:

We have just learned with profound sorrow of the death of your mother.

She was well-loved in this community for her charities and good work, and she will be long remembered by many.

We send you our heartfelt sympathy.

Sincerely yours,
Jan and Tom Stevens

Dear Mr. Owen:

All our thoughts are with you in this hour of grief. Mr. Graham joins me in sending deepest sympathy.

Sincerely,
Ethel Graham

My dear Owen:

I cannot tell you how sorry I am to hear of your great loss. Please accept my sympathy and best wishes.

Sincerely,
Jonathan P. Stevens

Dear Alice:

We just learned of the sudden death of your father. The shock was a great one. But he went as he would have wished—quickly and without suffering. That should be some consolation to you.

We send our deepest sympathy to you and your family. We hope that time will soon heal your sorrow.

Affectionately,
Leslie Blair

Dearest Alice:

I was so shocked to hear of your father's sudden death. My thoughts have been with you all day, as I know what your grief and sorrow must be. I wish there were something I could do or say to help.

You know you have my deepest sympathy—and my love and friendship always.

Affectionately,
Emily

Dear Alice:

I'm so very sorry to hear of the death of your father.

Please accept my profound sympathy. I hope you won't hesitate to call on me if there's anything I can do.

Affectionately yours,
Malcolm Cushing

Dear Mrs. Taylor:

It was a great shock to hear of your father's death. He was a wonderful neighbor and friend. and he'll be missed by many.

Mr. Henderson and I send kind thoughts and sympathy to you and your family.

Sincerely yours,
Agnes Henderson

Dear Mrs. Taylor:

We have heard the sad news and wish to offer our heartfelt sympathy.

You have the consolation of knowing your father went quickly, without suffering. That should help you bear the pain of his loss.

We send you and your family our affectionate regards—and deep regrets for this sudden and unexpected sorrow.

Sincerely,
Hellen and Frank Austin

Dear Jim:

I sympathize with you on the loss of your father, to whom I know you were deeply devoted.

I hope you will find what comfort you can in the fact that he was with you to a fine old age . . . and that you made his life such a happy one. He was so proud of you, Jim-so proud of your splendid accomplishments. That should help soften your sorrow a little.

Lillian joins me in sending affection and sympathy. You know that if there's anything we can do, you have only to tell us.

Sincerely,
Walter

Dear Jim;

Your father told me so many, many times what a rich, full life his had been—and how much more he had to be grateful for than most people. Let that be your consolation now. He was with you for a considerable part of your life; and you were able to make him very comfortable and happy.

You'll miss him, of course—as we all shall miss his friendly smile and gay spirits. But time will bring comfort in the memory of your many good years together. Try to think of that, Jim, and not of your loss.

Ted and the girls join me in sending wholehearted sympathy.

Affectionately yours,
Isabel

Dear Jim:

My thoughts are with you in your bereavement. You have my heartfelt sympathy. Is there anything an old friend can do to help?

Always sincerely,
Raymond

Dear Mr. Hartwell:

I have just learned of your loss and wish to offer my deepest sympathy.

I knew your father for many years, and always admired and respected him. He will be long and well remembered by his many friends.

Sincerely,
Russel T. Kirkwood

Dear Mr. Hartwell:

We were saddened to read of your father's death in this morning's paper. He was a fine old gentleman, well-loved and admired by all who knew him.

We can well appreciate your great sense of loss. But we hope you'll find some small measure of comfort in the good wishes and heartfelt- sympathy of your great host of friends-among whom I hope you include Mr. Travers and myself.

With affectionate regards from both of us,

Sincerely,
Marian Travers

Dear Mr. Hartwell:

Please accept my sincere condolences on the death of your father. I was indeed sorry to hear the sad news.

Sincerely yours,
Helen Blake

Dear Mr. Hartwell:

May old neighbors who remember your father with affection send you a message of sympathy?

We were greatly saddened by the news; and we can well imagine what your own grief must be. But we hope you'll find consolation in the monument of love and respect your father left behind in this community. You can be sure that no one who knew him will ever forget him.

With sympathy and best wishes,

Cordially yours,
Maud and Jules Galloway

ON THE DEATH OF A HUSBAND OR WIFE

If you have a particularly difficult letter of condolence to write, try to put yourself in the place of the person to whom you are writing. Try to imagine how you would feel under similar circumstances, and what you would like said to you at such a time. Then write as simply and briefly as you can. Remember that **tact**, **sincerity** and **brevity** are the essential qualities of a good letter of condolence. A long, wordy letter that needlessly stirs up the emotions of the bereaved is undesirable and unkind.

A message of sympathy to someone who has just lost a beloved husband or wife is especially difficult to write. The following examples may prove helpful when you are at a loss for words.

Dear Mary:

There are not enough words of comfort in any language for you now. I know that . . . and yet I must write and try to comfort you.

Darling you must not grieve. Arthur would not want you to grieve. He'd want you to bear up for the children's sake-and for your own.

I hope you can find a little comfort in the many friends who are thinking of you today, who love you and share your grief. There isn't anything I wouldn't do to help you, if I only could!

With love and heartfelt sympathy,

Susan

Mary, darling:

What can I say? What can **anyone** say? There just aren't words to express my overwhelming sorrow at your great loss.

I know you'll be fine and brave for the children's sake; and that you'll find comfort in the memory of the many happy years you shared with Arthur.

All my thoughts are with you, Mary. I only wish that sharing your grief could take some part of it away!

Love and deepest sympathy from Joe and myself,

Betty

Dear Mary:

We are shocked by the sad news. Is there anything Fred or I can do?

Our hearts are filled with sympathy for you in this hour of trial. We send you our love, and our assurance of devoted friendship-now and always.

Lillian

Dearest Mary:

No one knows better than I what you are thinking and feeling, for I have so recently gone through the same bitter experience.

I know well how meaningless words are to you now and how little even your best friends can do to comfort you. But time is a great healer, Mary—and it will soon soften the pain and bring you peace of mind. just as it did for me.

You have your children, Mary—and you can be very grateful for that. I am all alone. But I have my memories of my beloved husband, and they grow more precious to me with every passing day. You will have that too. my dear. You will have beautiful memories that no one can take away from you, **ever**.

So try and be brave these first difficult.weeks. I send you a heart full of sympathy and understanding; and you know you have my love always.

Janet

Dear Mrs. Bishop:

We feel for you in your great sorrow and send you our heartfelt condolences.

It should be some consolation to you to know that everyone who knew your husband admired and respected him. There are many in this community who will never forget him—Mr. Keeley and I among them.

We hope you will count us your friends as well as your neighbors, and call on us if there is ever anything we can do.

Sincerely yours,
Ida Keeley

Dear Mrs. Bishop:

I am profoundly sorry to learn of the death of your husband for whom I had the greatest admiration and regard.

Please accept my deepest sympathy.

Sincerely yours,
Gerald P. Searle

Dear Tom:

Words can't express our shock and grief at the sad news. We know how great your sorrow must be, but we beg you to bear up and be brave for your family's sake. You know Ellen would want you to. . . .

We send you our sympathy and affection in this hour of trial, and we hope you won't hesitate to call on us if there is anything we can do.

Fondly,
Kate and Charles

Dear Tom:

It was a great shock to hear of Ellen's death. I know that nothing I can say will help you; but I want you to know you have my heartfelt sympathy.

Affectionately,
Carl

Dear Tom:

The news of your great loss has just come to us. John and I realize what this means to you, and our hearts are filled with sorrow. Will you let us know if there is anything we can do to help?

With affection and deepest sympathy,

Laura

Dear Tom:

There's not much we can say at a time like this. But Marge and I want you to know how deeply we feel for you in your sorrow-and how much we would like to help. Will you call on us if there's anything we can do?

With profound sympathy,

Sincerely,
Jerry

Dear Tom:

Ellen was my best friend, and I loved her dearly. But it's with you that my thoughts are today, for I know how you must be grieving.

Ellen wouldn't want you to grieve, Tom. You know that, don't you? You made her very happy, always. She used to tell me you were the most wonderful husband in the world. Try to find some comfort in that -and in the memory of your many fine years together.

Will you have someone telephone me if there's anything you'd like me to do? George and I send you our affection and deepest sympathy in this dark hour.

Judith

Dear Mr. Bailey:

Mr. Comstock and I are profoundly sorry to hear of your great loss. We wish there were something we could do. If there ever is, now or in the future, will you count us your friends and call on us?

Sincerely yours,
Thelma Comstock

Dear Mr. Bailey:

It is with great sorrow that I have just learned of the death of your wife.

I know there is little I can say to lessen your grief; but I'd like you to know you have my deepest sympathy in your bereavement.

Sincerely yours,
Horace Mitchell

Dear Mr. Bailey:

Upon my return to New York today, I was shocked to learn of the death of Mrs. Bailey.

I can well realize what this great loss means to you, and I send my sincerest sympathy. I hope that time will quickly ease your sorrow.

With warmest personal regards,

Sincerely yours,
Erie Larkin

Dear Mr. Bailey:

News of Mrs. Bailey's death has just reached me, with all the attending shock such news carries.

May I add my little word of consolation to that of the countless who knew and admired her?

My husband asks to be included in these condolences.

Sincerely yours,
Florence Whitmore.

ON THE DEATH OF A CHILD

How heartbreaking the death of a child can be! And how.cruel a long, wordy message is at such a time, especially if it probes into the details of the child's illness or manner of death. It's far better not to write at all than to write carelessly or thoughtlessly to grief-stricken parents. Remember that the only purpose of a letter of condolence is to give comfort. It should sympathize and console . . . but it should not recall any memories nor stir up any emotions that increase the heartbreak. A note to bereaved parents should be short, very short-and should scrupulously avoid mention of any subject that could possibly give pain.

Dear Julia:

I'm thinking of you, darling . . . and hoping you'll be as brave as you've always been.

My love and deepest sympathy to you and David.

Affectionately,
Joan

Dearest Julia:

Our hearts are heavy today with the grief of your great

loss. Bob and I couldn't feel any worse if it were our own child.

We send you and David our most heartfelt sympathy. How we wish there were some way we could soften the blow and take away some of your sorrow!

Devotedly,
Florence

Julia, my dear:

We know only too well the shock and grief you and David are suffering today, for it's only a little more than a year since our own son was taken.

Our hearts are filled with sympathy for you both. We hope that time will soon ease the pain. In the meantime, Julia, you must be strong and brave—for the sake of David and the other children. They look to you for guidance and comfort.

With all our love,

Martha and Henry

Dear Julia:

There are no words to express our grief at the sad news. Our hearts are filled with sorrow for you and David.

Is there anything we can do? You know how grateful we'd be if you let us help in some way.

Joel and I send our love, and our deepest sympathy to you both.

Affectionately,
Charlotte

Dear Julia and David:

We know there's little consolation in a note, even from friends who love you well and share your grief.

But Fred and I want you to know our thoughts are with

you every minute; and there isn't anything we wouldn't do to ease your pain and sorrow if we only could!

We hope you'll try to bear up for the sake of the other children. They need your faith and courage to help them through this bad time.

With love to you all,

Affectionately,
Mabel

Dear David:

I've just heard the sad news, and I can't tell you how sorry I am.

You and Mrs. Tuttle have the heartfelt sympathy of all your friends here at Hall-Brent. We feel your loss keenly, and we wish there were some way we could lighten the burden of your great sorrow.

Will you let me know if there's anything I can do? I hope you know you can always count on my friend-ship and affection.

Sincerely,
Ted Baker

Dear Dave:

I was mighty sorry to hear about the little fellow. That's certainly bad news. My sympathy and kindest thoughts to you and Mrs. Tuttle.

Sincerely,
Jack Brady

Dear Mrs. Andrews:

I was shocked to hear of the great sorrow that has come to you and your household. I send my deepest sympathy to you and Mr. Andrews.

Sincerely,
Edna William

Dear Mrs. Andrews:

Mr. Davis and I are profoundly sorry to hear of your son's death.

We realize what a sad blow this has been; and we send you and Mr. Andrews our heartfelt sympathy. We wish it were within our power to soften your great sorrow.

Sincerely yours,
Rose Davis

Dear Mr. and Mrs. Andrews:

I hope you will forgive me for intruding on your grief. Although I'm a new neighbor and almost a stranger to you, I must tell you how deeply I feel for you in this great sorrow.

Mr. Mulhall and I extend to you our warmest sympathy. Please count us among those who share your grief and whose hearts are heavy for you today.

Sincerely yours,
Dorothy K. Mulhall

Dear Mr. Andrews:

I have just learned with deepest sorrow and regret of the death of your little boy.

I realize the inadequacy of words to comfort you in your great grief. But I'd like you and Mrs. Andrews to know my thoughts are with you in your bereavement; and I stand ready and eager to help in any way I can.

With sympathy and warmest personal regards,

Sincerely yours,
Edwin Corbett

ON THE DEATH OF A RELATIVE

When someone loses a relative, it's kind and thoughtful to write a brief note of sympathy. If you knew the person who died, you may want to include a word of praise in your message. Otherwise a simple expression of sympathy, a word or two of comfort, are all that are, necessary.

Dear Jim:

I know how devoted you were to your brother, and I just can't tell you how stunned and distressed I am by the sad news.

Please extend my sincere sympathy to your mother, and tell her how deeply I feel for her—and all of you—in this great sorrow.

Sincerely,
Margot Walsh

Dear Claire:

I wish I knew how to comfort you on the loss of your sister. She was so sweet and charming! No one who knew her will ever forget her.

But you must accept this great blow with courage, Claire—for the sake of your mother. She needs you so desperately now, and will look to you for comfort in the months ahead.

I send you both my love and deepest sympathy, and only wish it were possible to take away some of your grief.

Affectionately,
Celia

Dear Mrs. Phillips:

We were very sorry to hear of the death of your sister. Although she was very ill, and you were more or less prepared for it—we know how great your loss is and we sympathize with you in your bereavement.

Mr. Willard joins me in sending condolences to you and your family.

Sincerely yours,
Amy R. Willard

Dear Fred:

Your sister died as she lived, simply and quietly . . . with the love and respect of all who knew her.

I hope you are finding some small measure of comfort in the fact that she went quickly, without suffering.

But I know well how much you'll miss her. Fred, and I send you my deepest sympathy. Eleanor asks to be included in this message, and sends you her affectionate regards.

Sincerely,
Roger

Dear Mr. Forrest:

Word of the recent death of your brother has just come to me, and I hasten to offer condolences.

I had the privilege of knowing your brother in years past, and I realize your great loss. He was a fine and brilliant man, and he will not soon be forgotten by the many who admired and respected him.

Please convey my sympathy and my warm personal regards to all your family.

Cordially yours,
Gerald M. Larkin

Dear Paula:

I have just this moment learned of the sudden death of your brother, Eric. I can't tell you how shocked I am by this sad news. I know what he meant to you and your sister, and I send you both my deepest sympathy.

I'm sure that many hearts must be heavy with sorrow today; for I never knew anyone with such a host of friends as Eric. He'll be keenly missed by everyone who knew him.

Is there any way I can help, Paula? You know I would gladly do anything I can.

With love,
Emily

Dear Miss Travers:

I have just been told of your aunt's death, and knowing your devotion to each other, I realize what a great loss this is to you.

I'd like you to know how sorry Mr. Patton and I are; and how deeply we sympathize with you in your bereavement.

With kindest thoughts from us both,

Sincerely,
Jennifer R. Patton

Dear Mrs. Drummond:

We read in this morning's paper of the death of your talented young nephew. We share with many the shock and sorrow of this tragic news; and our heart go out in sympathy to you and your family.

Mr. Rankin and I send our heartfelt condolences and we hope you will find some consolation in the record of brilliant achievements he leaves behind him.

Sincerely yours,
Bessie G. Rankin

Dear Myra:

My brother just telephoned and told me your niece died this morning. I'm terribly sorry to hear this sad news. I knew she was desperately ill; but like everyone else, I hoped and expected she would recover.

Please extend my heartfelt sympathy to your family. If there is anything I can do, you know you have just to mention it.

Affectionately,
Doris

WHEN DEATH IS A RELEASE

There are times when death is clearly "for the best," and

may be looked upon almost as a blessing rather than a great sorrow. Under these circumstances, the expression of sympathy or condolence should be for the long illness or suffering of the deceased, rather than the immediate death.

Here are typical examples of such letters, written when death was a release from long and hopeless suffering.

Carol, dear:

All my thoughts are with you and your mother today. My heart is filled with sympathy for you both-for the long year of suffering, and for your sorrow now that Jean is gone.

I loved your sister, Carol; I'm sure you know that, I shall miss her more than I can say. But I know how she suffered this past year, and I'm grateful that her suffering is over at last. I try to find comfort in that thought, and I hope you will, too.

Affectionately,
Lucy

Dear Ted:

I can only repeat in this note what you already know: that Jim and I are profoundly touched by all the sorrow that has come to you in these past few years. Our thoughts and sympathies were always with you, for we knew how terribly Emma suffered-and how hopeless her condition was.

Be grateful that her long suffering is over, Ted—and try to feel, as all your good friends do, that it was for the best.

With all our affection,

Fondly,
Grace

Dear Mrs. Carleton:

Yours has been a long and tragic sorrow; and now that it is over at last, I am sure that time will soon bring comfort and peace.

Mr. Jamison and I want you to know how deeply we sympathize with you for all you have endured through the years and now. We assure you of our affectionate regard. and hope you will let us know if there is anything either of us can do-as neighbors and friends.

Sincerely yours,
Laura Jamison

Dear Dick:

You have been through a great deal these past few months, and all my thoughts and sympathies are with you now.

I hope you will look on Barbara's death as a release from cruel and hopeless suffering. John and I feel deeply for you in your present sorrow, but we are grateful that the long ordeal is over.

Try not to look back, Dick. You. have your two fine sons to think about. So keep your eyes on the future and the life that lies ahead.

Always affectionately,
Carolyn

Dear Mr. Winters:

When I learned of your wife's death today, I was not as shocked as I might have been if I had not known of her long and tragic illness.

I'm deeply sorry for all the grief and sadness you've had, now and in the past . . . and I offer my sincere condolences.

I hope, that time will quickly bring the peace of mind so long denied you.

With best wishes,

Sincerely yours,
Henry T. Bishop

WHEN SOMEONE IS KILLED OR COMMITS SUICIDE

When death strikes, cruelly and without warning, it leaves shock and anguish to those left behind. Only relatives and close friends should write; others should not intrude upon the horror and heartache of sudden death.

To a Woman Whose Husband Was Killed In an Automobile Accident

Dear Christine:

We are stunned, as all your friends are, by the tragic news. Jerry and I send you our heartfelt sympathy, and we beg you to let us help you in any way we can.

Will you have someone call us if there's anything we can do? In deepest sorrow and affection.

Yours devotedly,
Sue

To a Woman Whose Husband Was Killed in a Plane Crash

Dearest Mildred:

There are no words to express my shock and grief. I wish I were there to comfort you in your anguish.

Be brave, darling-for little Tommy's sake. You know that Bill would want you to carry on. I'll come to you as soon as I can.

With all my love, your heartbroken

Sally

To a Mother Whose Child Was Killed in a Street Accident

Mary, darling:

Ed and I are too grieved and shocked even to try and express our sympathy.

Our hearts are fillled with sorrow for you and Pete. We hope and pray that time will quickly soften this terrible blow.

We send you our love, and we're standing by to help in any way we can. Have someone call us darling, if you want us.

Devotedly,
Jane

To a Man Whose Wife Died In Childbirth

Dear Fred:

We're heartbroken by the sad news. We know there are no words to comfort you now; but we want you to know we're thinking of you every moment, in sorrow and devotion.

Bill and I hope you'll accept this cruel blow with the courage and faith Anne would expect of you—for the sake of the little one.

You know you can count on us, Fred—now and always—for any help within our power to give.

With love and sympathy,

Isabel

To a Woman Whose Parents Were Killed In a Railroad Accident

Dear Claudia:

I just can't believe the terrible news. I wish with all my heart I could help or comfort you in some way.

It may be some slight consolation to you to know that your grief is shared by everyone in Middletown.

With deepest sympathy to you in your great loss,

Affectionately,
Kathryn

To a Man Whose Wife Committed Suicide

Dear Roy:

How could this have happened to you, who least deserved it?

Your friends all know your love and tireless devetion to Lenore. Only the agony of her long and painful illness could have driven her to such madness.

So don't ever blame or reproach yourself, Roy dear. You did everything you could for her—and all your friends are filled with sympathy and affection for you in your trouble.

I hope you'll let me help if there's anything I can do. Alan joins me in sending love and heartfelt-sympathy.

Edith

To a Woman Whose Crippled Son Committed Suicide

Dearest Cora:

We all know the torment of grief you have suffered so bravely, for so many years—and we cherish and admire you for it.

This last great shock seems almost too much to bear; but time is a wonderful healer, Cora darling—and when the anguish is over and your pain has eased, you will have the comfort and peace of mind so long denied you.

For Paul is at rest, dear. His agony is over. You and Fred did everything humanly possible for him; and you must never, never reproach yourselves in any way.

Jim and I send you both all our love and sympathy in this dark hour. If there's anything we can do to help, you know you have only to tell us.

Devotedly,
Irene

SOME FAMOUS LETTERS OF CONDOLENCE

Often it helps, in writing your own lottors, to know what others have written to family and friends in time of tragedy or bereavement. Here, for example, is a beautiful and touching letter written by William Godwin to his daughter Mary on the death of her husband, Percy Bysshe Shelley. The young poet was drowned in a storm at sea. The letter is dated August 9,

My poor girl! What do you mean to do with yourself? You surely do not mean to stay in Italy? How glad I should be to be near you, and to endeavor by new expedients each day to make up for your loss! But you are the best judge. If Italy is a country to which in these few years you are naturalized, and if England is become dull and odious to you, then stay.

I should think, however, that now you have lost your closest friend your mind would naturally turn homewards, and to your earliest friend. Is it not so? Surely we might be a great -support to each other, under the trials to which we are reserved, What signify a few outward adversities, if we find a friend at home?

Above all, let me entreat you to keep up your courage. You have many duties to perform; you must now be the father as well as the mother; and I trust you have energy of character enough to enable you to perform your duties honourably and well.

Ever and ever most affectionately yours,

The day her beloved sister Emily was buried, Charlotte Bronte (the author of **Jane Eyre**) wrote in sorrow and tender understanding to a friend who had been close to them both:

The anguish of seeing her suffer is over; the spectacle of the pains of death is gone by; the funeral day is past. We feel she is at peace. No need now to tremble for the hard frost and the keen wind. Emily does not feel them.

Princess Alice of England, the devoted daughter of Queen Victoria, wrote the following letter to her mother on the anniversary of her father's death:

Darmsstadt, December11,

Beloved-precious Mama,—

On awakening this morning, my first thoughts were of you and of dear darling Papa! Oh, how it reopens the wounds scarcely healed, when this day of pain and anguish returns! This season of the year, the leafless trees, the cold light, everything reminds me of that time!

Happily married as I am, and with such a good, excellent and loving husband, how far more can I understand now the depth of that grief which tore your lives asunder!

Alice

When Charles Dickens' infant daughter died, his wife was ill . . . and he broke the tragic news to her gently, tenderly, in a letter that has become a classic of its kind. He didn't actually tell her the child was dead; he prepared her slowly for the shock, let her realize for herself that there Was no hope.*

> You would suppose her quietly asleep, but I am sure she is very ill, and I cannot encourage myself with much hope of her recovery. I do not (and why should I say I do to you, my dear?) I do not think her recovery at all likely.... Remember what I have often told you, that we never can expect to be exempt . . . from the afflictions of other parents. . . .

When Robert E. Lee was president of Washington

---

* *This is a merely a brief excerpt. For the complete letter see Schuster, A Treasury of the World's Great Letters, p. 307.*

College, a student was drowned-and he had the sad duty of writing a note of condolence to the boy's father. Here is the first paragraph of his letter:*

Washington College,
Lexington, Virginia.
March 19,

My dear Sir:

Before this you have learned of the affecting death of your son. I can say nothing to mitigate your grief or to relieve your sorrow, but if the sincere sympathy of his comrades and friends and of the entire community can bring you any consolation, I can assure you that you possess it in its fullest extent.

By far the most famous condolence letter ever written—and, in fact, one of the most famous letters in American history—is the one Abraham Lincoln wrote to Mrs. Lydia Bixby, consoling her on the loss of five sons in the Civil War.

Executive Mansion
Washington. Nov. 21.

To Mrs. Bixby. Boston, Mass.

Dear Madam.

I have been shown in the files of the War Department a statement of the Adjutant General of Massachusetts that you are the mother of five sons who have died gloriously on the field of battle. I feel how weak and fruitless must be any word of mine which shall attempt to beguile you from the grief of a loss so overwhelming. But I cannot refrain from tendering you the consolation that may be found in the thanks of the republic they died to save. I pray that our

---

* *From : Capt. Robert E. Lee,* ***Recollections and Letters of General Robert E. Lee*** *(New York: Doubleday & Co., Inc, 1919)*

Heavenly Father may assuage the anguish of your bereavement, and leave you only the cherished memory of the loved and lost, and the solemn pride that must be yours to have laid so costly a sacrifice upon the altar of freedom.

Yours very sincerely and respectfully

A. Lincoln

❑❑❑❑❑

Chapter X

NOTES OF SYMPATHY ON ILLNESS, INJURY, AND MATERIAL LOSS

NOT all letters of sympathy are written on the sad occasion of death. They are written also to cheer friends who are ill, or who have been injured in an accident. They are also frequently written to relatives or friends who have suffered material loss by fire, flood, theft or other unfortunate circumstances.

A note of sympathy, like a note of condolence, should be tactful and sincere. If the illness or loss is a relatively minor one, the letter may be written in a light and bantering vein. But when a person is gravely ill or has suffered a really serious loss, any attempt to be facetious is in very bad taste and should be avoided. Even though your bright and witty letter may be written with the best intentions in the world, to cheer the invalid or unhappy victim of misfortune, you can be sure it will be resented. For people take their troubles seriously, and expect you to do likewise.

That doesn't mean your note of sympathy should be gloomy or pessimistic. Quite on the contrary! It should bring courage and comfort to the person who receives it ...should be like a mental handclasp, warm and friendly, and filled with promise for the future.

It's not at all difficult to write a good note of sympathy— one you can be sure will be received with pleasure and appreciation-if you are able to put yourself in the place of the person to whom you are writing . Just try to imagine yourself gravely ill or injured. Try to imagine how you would feel if your valuables were stolen or your property destroyed by fire. Would you welcome jokes or bright sayings from your friends at such a time? Or would you want kindness and understanding-would you want sincere and well-meant sympathy?

Just write as you would like to be written to under the name unhappy circumstances, and your letter will give the comfort and cheer for which it is primarily intended.

TO THOSE WHO ARE ILL

Always try to write to a sick person as though complete recovery were just around the corner-and he, or she, will soon be up again, sound and well as ever. Minimize the illness, if you can; don't dramatize its seriousness. And just in case you think that's farfetched, here's an actual excerpt from a letter written to someone in my family:

> I'm so sorry to hear of your illness. I know how serious it is, because one of my best friends died of it.

Surely that's the perfect example of what not to say in a letter of sympathy!

The spirit behind your message should be, **Sorry to hear you're not well But you will he very soon, of course! Just want you to know I'm thinking of you....** Say it any way you like, but that should be the meaning behind your words. Unless a note of sympathy makes the person who receives it feel better—unless it gives that person a mental lift and a more cheerful outlook-it should be dropped into the wastebasket and not the mailbox! For a gloomy or thoughtless letter can do more harm than good to someone already depressed by illness or suffering.

A note of sympathy may be quite brief, just a paragraph or two. Or it may be long and chatty, like the letters you write to friends who are not ill. The length of the letter is not important. But what you say in your letter is very important indeed to the person confined to a lonely room, ill . . . and perhaps in pain. Your letter should be like a warm and friendly visit with that person, bringing brightness and cheer into the sickroom, bringing at least momentary escape from the loneliness or pain.

When writing to an invalid or convalescent you know well, try to bring the outside world to him by writing of the things in which he is interested and with which he is familiar. For example, if he's a golf enthusiast, tell him about the 90 your neighbor shot the other day. If his hobby is tropical fish, tell him about the exhibit you saw recently . . . or the article you read in a magazine . . . or the new kind of tank just developed for Siamese fighting fish. If necessary, go out of your way to get some interesting tidbit of information to include in your letter. Remember that you are able to get around and the sick person is not. He'll appreciate news of the outside world. especially in his own field or hobby.

To a woman whose great love is gardening, you might write about the flower show . . . or tell her how lovely her garden looked as you went by it that morning . . . or confide plans for your own garden next Spring. Or You might mention that you saw her children recently, and how lovely they looked-or how surprised you were to see how big they were getting. You can always find something to write about that's of interest to t he patient, if you really want to. If you are writing to someone who has no special interests or hobbies, you can always write about people. Everyone is interested in people: what they are doing, where they are going, what they have accomplished.

The following examples cover a variety of circumstances and are written with different degrees of intimacy. Some are formal and reserved in tone, but cordial-the type of notes you might write to neighbors or acquaintances with whom you are friendly but not intimate. Others are chatty and informal in tone, and are the type of notes you would send to relatives or close friends.

Bear in mind that the most important thing is to write **optimistically**, with the cheerful assumption that the sick person is well on the road to recovery.

Dear Mrs. Corbin:

I was so sorry to learn of your illness. You must hurry and get well! Everybody in the neighborhood misses you, and we're all hoping you'll be back soon.

Mr. Burke joins me in sending best wishes for your speedy recovery.

Sincerely yours,
Mary T. Burke

Dear Mr. Warner:

I was mighty sorry to hear you were in the hospital. But your son says you're making fine progress, and that's wonderful news to everybody around here!

Keep up the good work. Mrs. Johnson and I hope you'll regain your health and strength in record time, and that we'll soon see you back in your own house, as well as ever.

Until then, our very best wishes!

Cordially yours,
George Johnson

Dear Mr. Pratt:

Word of your illness has just reached Middletown, and your many friends here are thinking of you—and hoping for your quick return to health. We won't be content until we hear that you are completely recovered and yourself again!

I understand you will be in the hospital for a few weeks. I'm sending you some books to help make the time pass more quickly. I hope you'll enjoy reading them.

Mrs. Lawson sends her best wishes. We expect to see

you back in Middle town real soon, hale and hearty—and with all your old vitality!

Cordially yours,
Henry T. Lawson

Dear Miss Turner:

Your mother has just informed us of your emergency operation last Tuesday. We were surprised and very sorry to hear about it, but happy to know everything is progressing nicely and that you'll soon be up and around again.

We certainly hope your convalescence will be swift and uneventful, and that you'll be back with your family in no time.

With best wishes from all the Wheelers,

Sincerely yours,
Amy G. Wheeler

Dear Roger:

Yesterday Jim Ryan told me about your wife's illness. I am very sorry to hear about it, and I hope she will soon regain her health.

Please give her my sympathy and very best wishes.

Cordially,
Phil

Dear Dr. Howell:

Mrs. Dunne and I are extremely sorry to hear of your illness. We often wondered how you could keep going as you did, day and night. It was—bound to catch up with you sooner or later!

We do hope you won't rush your recovery—that you'll think of yourself, for a change, and get a good rest before you return to your practice. We're sending you some books we think you'll enjoy.

With best wishes for your quick and complete return to health,

Sincerely yours,
Gilbert Dunne

Dear Mr. Foster:

I'm delighted to hear that you are well on the road to recovery and will be able to leave the hospital in a week or so.

We've all missed you around here. It will be wonderful to see you up and around again—your old cheerful self!

With best wishes for a speedy convalescence,

Sincerely yours,
Elaine Falcon

Dear Edith:

We missed you so much at the meeting last week! You have no idea how much you mean to your many friends.

So hurry and lick that old flu germ, will you? Another meeting without you is **unthinkable**!

Your mother says you're feeling a lot better, and I'm so glad to hear it. But I hope you'll be entirely better by the time this note reaches you.

Did you hear about Elsie Keith? She won the prize for architectural design. Isn't that wonderful? She's going to New York next week to receive the award.

And, oh yes! Betty Larkin's engaged to Phil Walten. What do you think of a surprise shower for her at the club house? Don't you think it would be fun?

The girls asked me to send you their best wishes, Edith. We all hope you'll soon be completely well.

Affectionately,
Grace

Dear Joe:

I've just this minute heard that you are, in the hospital. I think you are very wise to find out once and for all what's causing your trouble, and get it over with.

I hope that by the time this note reaches you, you'll be feeling a great deal better. I'm sure that now it won't be long before you are entirely and completely yourself again.

By the way, Joe, the boys are postponing that fishing trip until you can join us. We've decided it wouldn't be nearly as much fun without you. So hurry and get well!

Affectionately,
Harry

Dear Mary:

I hear you are making such a rapid recovery that you'll soon be out of the hospital and back with your family and friends. That's wonderful news, Mary!

I've missed you so much. You've been on my mind constantly, ever since you went to the hospital. I just can't tell you how sorry I was that you had such a difficult time of it.

But all that's over now, and you'll soon be as good as new! I met Dr. Carleson at my sister's house yesterday (her little boy has the mumps) . . . and he tells me you are his prize patient. He says you rallied beautifully, and that from this point on you'll show steady improvement—until you have all your old health and strength back again.

I saw John yesterday, too. The poor man is like a lost sheep without you! He says he's counting the very hours until you come home. Janet was with him; my, how she has grown in the past year! You have a lovely daughter, Mary . . . as gracious and charming as she is sweet to look at. You must be very proud of her.

This morning I walked by your house on the way to the

post office, and I lopped for a moment to look at your garden. I still say it's the most beautiful garden in town! Your roses are magnificent this year. And I do hope you'll get home before the lilacs are gone—they're simply **gorgeous!**

Frank sends his best wishes, and he says to be sure and tell you how delighted he is to hear about your fine progress. Keep it up, Mary—and come home real soon to those who love and miss you.

Affectionately,
Lillian

TO THOSE WHO HAVE BEEN INJURED

A note written to someone who has been injured in an accident should be as brief as possible, and genuinely sympathetic. It is better not to write at all than to write out of curiosity. The spirit behind your message should not be, "How did it happen? Whose fault was it? Were there any witnesses?"—but "I'm so sorry to hear about it! I hope you weren't badly injured and that you'll soon be all right again." In other words, your concern should not be for the details of the accident but for the condition and well-being of the person who has been injured.

Dear Miss Jenkins:

I was indeed sorry to hear of your fall, and of the injury to your hip. I am told it's not a very serious injury, and I'm sure that's as great a relief to your family as it is to your many friends.

I sincerely hope you will make a quick recovery, and that you'll soon be up and around again—as well as ever!

Cordially yours,
Vincent R. Mitchell

Dear Mrs. Farrell:

My husband and I were shocked and distressed to read

about tli- terrible accident in which you were involved. We were somewhat cheered, however, to learn from your son that you were not among the more seriously injured.

Please accept our sympathy on your unfortunate experience, and let us know if there's anything we can do to help. We hope you are already on the mend, and that you'll soon be completely recovered from your injuries.

Sincerely yours,
Natalie Collins

Dear Mr. Brown:

I met your brother today, and he told me about the accident you had. I'm certainly sorry to hear about it.

I understand that your injuries are painful, but not serious—and that you'll be able to leave the hospital in about a week. That, at least, is something to be thankful for!

If I can be of any service, will you let me know? In the meantime, I'm sending some books and puzzles to help pass the time until you are well enough to go home.

My sympathies to you, and best wishes for a speedy recovery.

Sincerely,
Bert Clifford

Dear Tom:

I just can't tell you how sorry I was to learn of your accident. Your family tells me that you are progressing nicely, and that you'll be out of the hospital in about ten days. I'm certainly relieved to know that!

In the next day or so you'll receive a little package-from Margaret and me. I hope you like it, and that it will help to pass the time more pleasantly.

With every good wish for your swift recovery,

Sincerely,
Bob

Dear Ruth:

It was certainly a shock to read in last night's **Press** that you were injured in an automobile accident and taken to the hospital.

Mother and I were terribly upset about it. We hope that your injuries are not serious and that you will soon be up and around again. We won't come until we're sure that you want visitors; but in the meantime we'll keep in touch with Ellen so we'll know how you are getting along.

We send you our love and our sympathy, Ruth. We're sorry you were hurt, and we won't be content until we hear that you are completely well again.

Affectionately,
Phyllis

Dear Mrs. Gilbert:

I feel I simply **must** write these note and tell you how much you are in the hearts and minds of everyone in Middle town.

We were shocked and saddened beyond words by news of the crash. But we were grateful, too, that your injuries were not worse.

The affection and best wishes of the entire town are with you, and everyone's hoping for your quick and complete recovery.

Sincerely yours,
Cora Stanley

Dear Marjory:

I've just learned that young Pete was hurt in a football game. I'm ever so sorry to hear it, and I hope his injuries are not serious.

I know just how you feel because I had the same experience with George a few years ago—remember?

I guess it's just something all mothers of growing boys must expect!

Please let me know if there's anything I can do to help. Perhaps you'd like to send Patsy here for a week or so, until Pete is better. We'd love to have her, and I'd see that she got to and from school safely. Just phone me, Marj—and I'll come and get her.

Tell Pete I'm sorry he was hurt, and that I hope he'll soon be fit as a fiddle again.

Affectionately,
Harriet

Dear Mr. Willet:

I was extremely sorry to hear about Mrs. Willet's accident. I hope it is not serious, and that she will soon be entirely well again.

Please give her my very best wishes.

Sincerely yours,
Jonathan Kent

TO THOSE WHO HAVE SUFFERED MATERIAL LOSS OR DAMAGE

People who have suffered material loss or damage generally appreciate a brief message of sympathy from their friends. But it should not be a probing letter, filled with questions—a letter prompted more by curiosity than kindness. It should merely express sympathy, and perhaps offer help. Here are a few examples:

Dear Mr. Thompson:

I was extremely sorry to hear of the fire which destroyed your beautiful house in Far Acres. I know well how much that house meant to you and Mrs. Thompson, and I hasten to offer my sympathy.

With best wishes to you both,

Sincerely yours,
Roger Whitney

Dear Madeline:

I can't believe the lovely little cottage in Cornwall is gone! I was shocked and grieved when Bill told me about the fire. But he says you've been an awfully good sport about it—as, of course, you would be! You're always such a good sport, about everything.

Some day you and Bill will have another cottage to take its place. And in the meantime you have your memories of all the many happy summers you spent at Cornwall. Nothing can ever take that away from you, Madeline! I know **I'll** never forget the wonderful times I've had there as your guest.

All my love to you, dear—and my sympathy for what I know is a great loss to you and Bill.

Affectionately,
Cora

Dear Sally:

Your sister phoned this morning and told us about the fire which damaged your house last night. Jim and I know how distressing this experience can be, as we went through it ourselves. If there's any way we can help, will you call on us? You are more than welcome to use our basement for storing things until the damage to your house is repaired.

We hope the damage is less than you think, and that your lovely house will soon be good as new again.

Sincerely,
Betsy Wall

Dear Tom:

I've just heard about the great damage to your house

and grounds by the recent heavy floods in Middletown. I'm certainly sorry about it, and I wish you'd let me help if there's anything I can do.

I realize that words are little consolation at a time like this. But I'd like you to know that I'm thinking of you, Tom . . . that you and your family have my deepest sympathy in your trouble . . . and that you can count wholeheartedly on my friendship, now and always.

So will you let me know what I can do—how I can help'?

Affectionately,
Bill Stevens

Dear Mrs. Smithfield:

All your friends are shocked and grieved by the great loss suffered by your family in the recent flood. To lose a lovely home so cruelly and suddenly is a tragic experience, and no letter can adequately express our sympathy for you.

But there is at least some consolation in the fact that you and your family are safe. We knew that your house was directly in the path of the flood; and you can't imagine how relieved and grateful we were to hear that you had reached your sister's house safely and had escaped the full fury of the storm.

All your many friends and former neighbors in Middletown are anxious to help in every way possible. We are sending a box of blankets, sweaters, warm socks and other things you may need to help you through the emergency. We are also sending some books and toys to help cheer the children and keep them from thinking too much about their unhappy experience.

Will you tell us what else we can do? In the meantime, we send you our best wishes—and we hope you will meet this cruel but temporary setback with the courage and faith we know you possess.

Sincerely yours,
Anna G. Sloan
(For the Mothers' Club of Middletown)

Dear Mr. Arnall:

Your brother has told me of the heavy loss you suffered in the hurricane that brought so much destruction to your city last week.

I'm sincerely sorry to hear about it, and I hope you'll call on me if there's any way I can help in the emergency.

Mrs. Price joins me in sending sympathy and beat wishes to you and your family.

Cordially yours,
Henry M. Price

Dear Agatha:

I was dismayed to read about the robbery in this morning's paper. I know what your collection of jade means to you, quite apart from its material value. I certainly hope that the police catch up with the thieves and get the collection back.

All my sympathy to you in this unhappy experience!

Affectionately,
Joyce

Dear Ted:

I hear that thieves broke into your house and got away with a lot of valuables. That's certainly bad news. But I'm glad you and Jean weren't in the house at the time as you might have suffered personal injury. That would have been much more distressing to your many friends!

So don't let it get you down, Ted. Maybe the police will recover your property. And if not, I'm sure you and Jean will take the loss in your stride and not let it distress you too much.

Sincere sympathy to you both, and my best wishes—now and always!

Affectionately,
Steve

TO THOSE WHO HAVE LOST A WELL-LOVED PET

Under ordinary circumstances, it is not necessary to write a note of sympathy to a friend whose cat has died, or whose dog has been run over. But if the cat or dog is a well-loved member of the family (as so many pets are!) it's kind and thoughtful to write a few words of consolation to the person who most keenly feels the loss.

Dear Diane:

Bill just told me about Chipper, and I'm so sorry to hear about it.

I know how precious that little golden-throated canary was to you, and how badly you must feel. But Chipper lived to a good old age, Diane. Surely you couldn't have expected to keep him much longer....

So cheer up, and think of the **new** canary Bill promised to get for you. Let's both try to think of a cute name for it!

Fondly,
Leonore

Dear Emily:

I've just heard about Mitzie. She was such a beautiful cat, and such a loyal and devoted companion! I can well imagine how much you'll miss her.

But cats can't live forever, Emily—not even **very special** cats like Mitzie! She was getting quite old you know. So try not to feel too badly about losing her. You wouldn't have enjoyed watching her get more and more feeble.

With affection, and sincere sympathy to you in your loss,

Sincerely,
Susan

Alan, dear:

Your mother has just told me about Puck. Please don't feel too badly about it! Cruel things like that sometimes happen and we must learn to face them bravely.

It was an unfortunate accident, but no one was to blame—except, perhaps, poor little frisky Puck himself. I understand he ran right out under the wheels and was gone before you could even shout his name. So at least he didn't suffer, Alan—and that's something to be grateful for.

This morning I went to the kennels where I bought Puck for your birthday. They have one of his brothers there—a friendly, affectionate little dog with the funniest spot on his nose you ever saw! I fell in love with him at first sight, and I know you will, too. Will you come and look at him with me tomorrow after school? And if you like him, he's yours!

So cheer up, Alan darling. I'll call for you tomorrow at four. And on the way to the kennels, I'll tell you the wonderful, wonderful name I've thought of for your new dog

With love,
Aunt Lillian

❑ ❑ ❑ ❑ ❑

Chapter XI

LETTERS OF INTRODUCTION

The purpose of a social note of introduction is to bring together people you feel reasonably sure will find pleasure and enjoyment in each other's company.

For example, if you have a friend going to a distant city where you have other friends—and if you believe it would be mutually pleasant and agreeable for these people to meet—you offer to write a note of introduction. Or if someone you know and like is going to Nassau for a vacation and you happen to have very good friends who live in Nassau, you might say: "Be sure to stop in and see the Ridgways! I know you'll enjoy meeting them. Here—I'll give you a letter of introduction."

Notice that the letter is offered, not requested. No one should ever **ask** for a letter of introduction—nor should anyone write such letters carelessly or indiscriminately. It's an unkindness to your distant friend to give a letter of introduction to someone you do not know well . . . someone who may turn out to be a nuisance or a bore. It's equally inadvisable to send a letter of introduction to a casual acquaintance . . . someone who may not be at all interested in meeting your friend and who may look upon your letter as a presumption.

So make it a point never to write a letter of introduction unless you know both persons intimately and well. Even then, write it only if you feel sure that the meeting will be of interest or benefit to both of them. Ask yourself if the persons concerned have anything in common. Ask yourself if they would really enjoy meeting each other—if they are likely to get along easily and well together. If there is any doubt in your mind, don't write a letter of introduction.

For bear in mind that an introduction by letter imposed obligations and responsibilities far more binding than any spoken introduction. It's a demand upon a distant friend's courtesy, hospitality and time—a demand that cannot be denied without repudiating the friendship of the person who wrote the letter, and bluntly ignoring the person who presented it.

Before you write any letter of introduction, therefore. be sure that your friend wants it—and be sure that the person to whom it is written will want to receive it. Then write it briefly and to the point. It should give the name of the person being introduced—the reason or purpose for the introduction—and any other information that is relevant or important. As it is actually a letter of request, asking that kindness and hospitality be shown to a complete stranger, it should include an expression of thanks for any courtesies extended.

A letter of introduction may either be handed to the friend for whom it is written, to be presented personal—or it may be sent through the mail like any other letter. If it is to be delivered personally, the envelope should be left unsealed. Obviously nothing of an intimate nature should be included in a letter given to one friend for presentation to another. However a second and private letter may be written and sent by mail giving more information about the person who is on the way with a letter of introduction. Examples of these various types of letters follow.

TO BE PRESENTED IN PERSON

Dear Jim:

The bearer of this note. Mr. Robert Mitchell, of Chicago, plans to be in Asheville for about a month. Besides being a personal friend of mine, he is radio director of a number of top-ranking shows; and knowing how interested you are in radio advertising, I'm sure you'll enjoy meeting him.

I have long wanted you and Bob to know each other, and I'm glad of this opportunity to bring you together. I'll appreciate anything you can do to make Bob's stay in Asheville more enjoyable-and I know he will, too.

With kindest regards to you and Ellen,

Cordially yours,
Kenneth Dawson

Dear Elsie:

This will introduce Janet Blake who is going to spend the winter in Washington gathering material and doing research for a new book. She plans to spend her days at the Congressional Library, and her evenings with congenial people. I told her I know of no one more congenial than you!

I'm sure you'll like Janet, and that you two will enjoy each other's company immensely. I don't need to tell you how much I'll personally appreciate any courtesies you show her.

Sincerely yours,
Edith Preston

Dear Catherine:

I'm giving this letter to Gerald Breen, a very good friend of ours. He is going to be in Chicago for a few days, and I'd like you two to meet as you happen to be interested in the same thing: child welfare.

Mr. Breen is making a study of juvenile delinquency, and I told him about the wonderful work you are doing among the underprivileged children of Chicago. He is very eager to talk with you about it.

I'm sure you'll enjoy meeting Mr. Breen, and I'm equally sure he'll be delighted and charmed to meet you.

Affectionately,
Alice.

Dear Mr. Thompson:

This note will introduce James Fenton, of whom you've heard me speak many times. I've always been most anxious for you two to meet, as you have so many interests and hobbies in common that I feel sure you'll enjoy knowing each other.

Mr. Fenton will be in Middletown next week, and I've made him promise to look you up. He hesitated to "impose on a stranger," as he called it; but I pointed out that each of you has heard me talk about the other so often that you are practically acquainted! Besides, you are both chess experts—and for that reason alone you should meet!

I will appreciate any courtesy you show Mr. Fenton during his brief stay in Middletown, and I am sure he will too.

Please give my best wishes to Mrs. Thompson. I hope to see you both again before very long.

Sincerely yours,
Arthur T. Rhinelander

Dear Mrs. Hathaway:

The young lady, who hands 'you this note is Miss Virginia Andrews—the daughter of one of my oldest and dearest friends. She will be in New York for the next year or so to study fashion design.

Virginia is a charming and talented girl, and I feel so certain you will enjoy her company that I have insisted that she call and present this note. She has never been in New York before; and I'll be very grateful for any help or advice you can give her. I know she too will deeply appreciate any courtesy.

Very sincerely yours,
Martha B. Emmons

Dear Bill:

I am writing this letter for my good friend and former neighbor, John Larkin. He and Mrs. Larkin are moving to Cleveland, and will live within walking distance of your house.

I know that you and Wilma will like the Larkins very much . . . and I know they'll like you. That's why I am writing this letter. I think you should meet—not because I happen to be a mutual friend, but because you have so many interests in common. The Larkins are musical. They are excellent bridge players. They love to entertain. But I'll let you and Wilma discover all their many other neighborly charms and qualities for yourselves!

By the way, didn't you once tell me your daughter was interested in writing radio scripts? Well, get her to talk with John about it. John used to teach radio writing at Middle town University.

Thanks, Bill, for any kindness you may extend to the Larkins on my account. I feel certain you'll soon love them for themselves, and that before long you and they will become the very good neighbors and friends we have always been here in Middletown.

With best wishes to the family from all of us,

Affectionately,
Bruce

TO BE SENT BY MAIL

When a letter of introduction is sent by mail, it imposes less of an obligation on the person who receives it. For example, if you write to a distant friend and say, "My former neighbors, the Boltons, are going to live in your city and I think you'd enjoy knowing them"—it's up to the distant friend to decide whether or not she wants to know them. She takes the initiative, saving the newcomer this embarrassment.

And in as much as the letter was not, presented personally, she is free to make advances or not, as she feels inclined.

Deaf Peggy:

I've just learned that old friends of mine, Jane and Ira Hall, are now living in Chicago, at 70 Lake Shore Drive. That's practically next door to you, isn't it?

The Halls are very charming people, and I think you would enjoy knowing them. I told them all about you; so if you call them, they'll recognize the name right away and know who you are.

I hope you **will** call them, Peggy. They're really wonderful people to know, and lots of fun to be with. Bob and 1 have certainly missed them since they moved away!

When are you and Fred coming to New York again? It seems ages since we saw you!

Affectionately,
Lorraine

Dear Harry:

I have often spoken to you about Phil Evans and the many interests you and he have in common . . . even to the point of both of you having sons at Exeter. And you've often said you'd like to meet him.

So I'm writing this note to let you know Phil is in New York for a few weeks and is stopping at the Hampshire House. If you call him there, I'm sure he'll be delighted to arrange a meeting. He knows who you are and will recognize the name when you call.

I know how busy you are, Harry, and I realize that this suggestion may come at a very inopportune time. So please don't regard it as an obligation. But if you have any free time while Phil's in New York, do try to see him—as I'm sure both of you will thoroughly enjoy the meeting.

Cordially yours,
Charles Benton

Dear Joe:

My brother-in-law, Roy Fowler, will be in Boston all next week—at the Statler Hotel. I've often wanted you two to meet, and this seems like the ideal opportunity.

Roy is research director of an advertising agency. I told him about the book you are writing on the history of buying trends in America, and he was completely fascinated—as I knew he would be! He said he'd like to know more about it., and I think you might find it interesting and helpful to discuss it with him.

So call him if you can, Joe—but not if it's an inconvenience. If he doesn't hear from you, he'll understand that it's because you are tied up. I suggest this meeting only because I know you two are bound to enjoy each other's company.

Cordially,
Homer

Dear Marcia:

I was interested to hear that you and Bill will be at the Whitehall in Forest Beach during the month of February. My sister and her husband will be there at the same time—and you simply **must** meet them as I know you'll all enjoy one another's company.

My sister is Mrs. Wilbur J. Sloan. She used to be Janet Turner, the swimming star, She and her husband are excellent bridge players; and they play the same kind of golf as you and Bill—in the low 90's.

I've already written to Janet and told her that you will be there. She'll be expecting you to ask for her at the desk or to leave a message in her box. She has heard me speak of you many times, Marcia, and she's most anxious to meet you.

I **do** hope you'll get together, as I know you'll enjoy being with the Sloans as much as they'll enjoy being with **you**. Have a wonderful time!

Affectionately,
Barbara T. Owen

"FOLLOW UP" LETTERS OF INTRODUCTION GIVING ADDITIONAL INFORMATION

Frequently when a letter of introduction is given to a friend to be delivered in person, another letter is written at the same time and sent by mail. The purpose is to say that the letter of introduction is on the way . . . and to give any additional information that may seem necessary or desirable. Here are some examples of such "follow up" letters:

Dear Jim:

In the next day or so you will receive a telephone call from Robert Mitchell of Chicago. He is a very good friend of mine; and as he is planning to be in Asheville for a month or more, I gave him a letter of introduction to you.

I know how busy you are, Jim, and I don't want you to regard this as an obligation. But I feel certain you'll enjoy meeting Bob Mitchell; and I'll wager that once you meet him, you'll want to keep on seeing him! For Bob's good company anywhere—at bridge, golf, tennis, or just talking. I should say **especially** talking! Bob's just about the most brilliant and entertaining conversationalist I know.

I'm writing this note so that you'll know who Bob is when he calls. I'll appreciate any kindness you and Ellen may show him as a stranger in Asheville; but please don't put yourselves out or feel that you are committed in any way at all. If I didn't feel you'd be as delighted to meet Bob as he will be to meet you, I wouldn't have given him a letter,

I hope you and Ellen are well, and I look forward to seeing you on your next visit to Chicago.

Sincerely yours,
Kenneth Dawson

Dear Elizabeth:

Our very good friend, Harvey Cromwell, will be in New York for the month of June—before going abroad to make a survey of housing conditions in England and France.

I have given him a note of introduction to you. Jim and I will deeply appreciate anything you can do to make his brief stay in New York pleasant.

Affectionately,
Margaret

Dear Mrs. Carter:

Dr. James Gibson will be in Buffalo the week of June tenth to attend the medical conferences. I am giving him a note of introduction to you.

Dr. Gibson has been our family physician for many years and we are utterly devoted to him. He is a talented musician as well as the best-loved doctor in town . . . and that's why I'd like you two to meet. I know you'll enjoy his playing as much as he enjoys your singing. He and Mr. Carter have an interest in common, too—as they are both ardent golfers. Perhaps they can manage a game together during Dr. Gibson's brief stay in Buffalo.

At any rate, I'd like you to know who Dr.Gibson is so that you'll recognize the name when he calls. I'm sure you and Mr. Carter will find much pleasure in making his acquaintance. And I know he'll thoroughly enjoy meeting both of **you!**

Needless to say, I'll deeply appreciate anything you may do to make Dr. Gibson's first visit to Buffalo more interesting and pleasant.

Cordially,
Edna B. Whitmore

Dear George:

A former neighbor of ours, Edward Brockton is moving

to Evanston in about a week or so I gave him a letter to you, as I think you'll enjoy knowing him.

Ed is a commercial artist, and a very good one. As a hobby he makes fascinating animated movies for children. You must get him to show them to your youngsters some time; they'll have them!

I'm writing this note so you'll know a little more about the Brocktons than my letter of introduction tells you. They're really grand people, George—and I know you and Jane will like them very much. They were our neighbors in Middletown for more than eight years, and we were mighty sorry when they moved away.

I feel certain that when you get to know the Brocktons they'll become your very good friends—as they are ours.

Thelma sends best wishes to you, Jane and the children.

Cordially,
Jim Tyler

Dear Catherine:

You will receive a call, in a few days, from a Mr. Gerald Breen. Fred and I have known him for many years and are very fond of him. He expects to be in Chicago for a short time, and we have asked him to get in touch with you. He has a letter of introduction.

Mr. Breen is a lawyer who is especially interested in juvenile delinquency and child welfare. He has an article in this month's **Sentinel** called "Are Parents Delinquent, Too?" I told him all about you, and the work you are doing among the underprivileged children of Chicago—and of course he's extremely interested. He said he'd like very much to talk with you about it while he's in Chicago and has the opportunity.

So will you see him if it's convenient, Catherine—and tell him whatever you can? I'm sure you'll enjoy meeting him; he's interesting and very likable.

When are you coming to New York again? We had such fun last time you were here that we're looking forward with great pleasure to your next visit.

Affectionately,
Alice

A FAMOUS LETTER OF INTRODUCTION

The following letter of introduction was written by the gifted composer, Felix Mendelssohn, to a friend in London. Although it was written more than a hundred years ago, it has none of the pompous phraseology of that period . . . and remains the classic letter of its kind: simple. charming and very much to the point.*

Berlin, March 10,

My dear friend,

The bearer of these lines, although a boy of thirteen, is one of my best and dearest friends and one of the most interesting people I have met for a long time. His name is Joseph Joachim. He was born in Hungary at Pesth, and he is going to London.

Of all the young talents that are now going about the world, I know none that is to be compared with this violinist. It is not only the excellence of his performances, but the absolute certainty of his becoming a leading artist—if God grants him health and leaves him as he is—which makes me feel such an interest in him. . . .

He is not yet very far advanced in composition, but his performances of the Vieuxtemps, Bruch and Spohr concertos, his playing at sight (even the second violin parts of difficult quartets I have heard him play in the most masterly

---

* G. Selden-Goth, **Flex Mendelssohn-Bartholdy Letters** (New York; Pantheon Books, Inc., 1945).

manner), his accompanying of sonatas, etc., is in my opinion as perfect and remarkable as may well be.

I think he will become a yeoman in time, as both of us are. So pray, be kind to him, tell him where he can hear good music, play to him, give him good advice, and for everything you may do for him, be sure that I shall be as much indebted to you as possible. Farewell.

Very truly yours,
F.M.B.*

❐ ❐ ❐ ❐ ❐